Arthur Tappan Pierson

Keys to the word;

Or, help to Bible study

Arthur Tappan Pierson

Keys to the word;
Or, help to Bible study

ISBN/EAN: 9783337808587

Printed in Europe, USA, Canada, Australia, Japan

Cover: Foto ©Lupo / pixelio.de

More available books at **www.hansebooks.com**

KEYS TO THE WORD;

OR,

HELP TO BIBLE STUDY.

BY

A. T. PIERSON D. D.

NEW YORK:
LENTILHON & COMPANY,
150 FIFTH AVENUE.

COPYRIGHT, 1887, BY
ANSON D. F. RANDOLPH & COMPANY.

TO

EDWARD NORTH, L.H.D.,

Professor of the Greek Language and Literature in Hamilton College,

WHO,

WITH THE CULTURE OF THE ATHENIAN SCHOLAR, BLENDS THE CONSECRATION OF THE CHRISTIAN TEACHER,

AND

Whose contagious enthusiasm in the Greek tongue, and child-like reverence for the Holy Scriptures,

FIRST INSPIRED IN THE AUTHOR A DESIRE AND DETERMINATION TO READ THE WORD OF GOD IN THE ORIGINAL,

THIS HUMBLE ATTEMPT TO UNLOCK SOME OF ITS HIDDEN BEAUTIES

IS AFFECTIONATELY AND GRATEFULLY

INSCRIBED.

INTRODUCTION.

THE LAWS OF BIBLE STUDY.

BACK even of Genesis there is still a beginning, in the adoption of proper methods of Bible study, which should be considered at the outset. The Bible itself gives emphatic directions for its proper examination. First of all we are to remember that as the Book of God, inspired by the Holy Spirit, it demands, for its true perusal, a mind illumined by that same Spirit. Goethe says, that before a reader complains of obscurity in an author, he should examine whether he himself is "clear within; in the twilight a very plain writing is illegible." "The natural man receiveth not the things of the Spirit of God, neither can he know them because they are spiritually discerned." No amount of light on the pages will compensate for a blind eye. "If the light that is in thee be darkness, how great is that darkness!" The Bible should be taken up with the prayer, "*Open Thou mine eyes, that I may behold wondrous things out of Thy law.*"

This must be emphasized at the very threshold. No man can have spiritual insight into the Word of God without the influence of the illumining Spirit. The most able commentators have been the most devout. Bengel, author of "The Gnomon," bathed his studies in tears and hallowed them with prayers. Unless taught of the Holy Ghost, the Bible is a sealed book even to the learned.

This being assumed, three direct rules are found in the Word of God for its successful study:

"SEARCH," "MEDITATE," "COMPARE."

1. *Search* (Jno. v. 39): There is a great deal of listless, careless reading. Coleridge divided readers into four classes. The first class he compares to "an *hour-glass;* their reading being as the sand, it runs in and runs out, and leaves not a vestige behind. A second class resembles a *sponge*, which imbibes everything and returns it in nearly the same state. A third class is like a *jelly-bag*, which allows all that is pure to pass away, and retains only the refuse and dregs. The fourth class, like the slave of Golconda, cast aside all that is worthless, preserving only the pure gems." Or perhaps we might compare this fourth class to the *gold-pan* used for retaining the pure metal while the refuse is washed out. The only profitable reading of God's Word is a *searching* reading. The word translated "*search*,'

is emphatic and intense: it literally means to "look carefully," as a wild animal searches the sands to find the footsteps of a stray cub. The Bible is full of hidden treasures, to be sought as the merchantman sought goodly pearls. They are not revealed to indifferent and superficial readers.

The true beauty of a Scripture passage does not lie on the surface, nor reveal itself to a careless eye. A fragment of spar, which at first seemed lustreless and unattractive, as you turn it in your hand, and let the light strike it at a certain angle, reveals beautiful radiance and even prismatic colors. A fragment of Scripture which is comparatively dull and dead to a superficial reader, becomes, in the hand of a devout student, a marvel of beauty. He turns it round and round, views it at every angle, till he sees the light of God break through it, and it shines with the sevenfold beauty of the divine attributes. Michael Angelo, on examining the work of one of his students, took his pencil and wrote on it the one word—"amplius"—wider. That word needs to be written over all our Scripture studies.

2. *Meditate* (Psalm i. 2): The process of prayerful reflection,—prolonged and concentrated thinking,—is the secret of true knowledge of the Word. There is a process of infusing, suffusing, transfusing the whole nature with

the divine Word, and it consists in devout meditation. The whole nature should be immersed in the Scriptures till they penetrate and permeate our whole being; till the mind is saturated with holy thoughts, the heart with holy affections, the memory with holy associations. This enables us to overcome evil with good.

Dr. Chalmers, riding on a stage-coach, by the side of the driver, said: "John, why do you hit that off leader such a crack with your lash?" "Away yonder," said he, "there's a white stone, that off leader is afraid of that stone; so, by the crack of my whip and the pain in his legs, I want to get his idea off from it." Dr. Chalmers went home, elaborated the idea, and wrote "The Expulsive Power of a New Affection."

Great is the expansive and expulsive power of the Word of God when it indwells in the soul. Preoccupation is the true law of possession and conquest. The mind filled with God's own truth has no room for inferior, and especially for defiling, thoughts. Temptation has no hold upon a heart already thrilled with the love of things divine. Meditation on the Word of God begets that spiritual mind which is the very opposite of the carnal mind, and the secret of life and peace.

3. *Compare* (1 Cor. ii. 13): Dr. A. J. Gordon likens Scriptural teachings to a dissected picture, the fragments of which are scattered through

the Word, needing to be brought together, laid side by side, matched and jointed, that they may present one complete view of truth. Let the careful student make trial of this method, and he will find not only the highest pleasure, but the highest profit. Almost any heresy may borrow apparent sanction from isolated Scripture texts, and so "even the Devil can cite Scripture to his purpose"; but when spiritual things are compared with spiritual, they mutually complete, vindicate, and illustrate each other.

Take, for instance, *"Life Eternal"* as set forth in the Gospel according to John. Begin with the first mention of Life, in the fourth verse of the first chapter, and follow the process and progress of development of the grand thought and theme till you reach chapter twentieth, verse thirty-first, where all the teachings of that sublime Gospel are summed up in one sentence; and there will be found, at every new stage of progress, some new and beautiful addition to the complete truth. You are reminded of the story of Michael Angelo and the "sleeping cupid," whose disjointed members had been separated and buried, and were again brought together in one beautiful statue.

These are the general principles upon which the Word of God itself counsels the earnest reader to pursue his study.

Beside these there are some obvious methods for successful mastery of the contents of the Bible which ought to be carefully observed.

Among them all none is of more importance than to find out *the exact purpose and object of each book.* To know who wrote it, where and when it was written, in what circumstances and for what end, is to throw a flood of light upon every chapter and verse. Bishop Percy therefore says, that "To understand the specific use of each book is the best commentary, and often makes needless any other." It is like a guidebook or map of a country in the aid it furnishes the traveler.

Having found the meaning of any book, as a whole, we are prepared to *examine into details*, to search into each verse, and ascertain its relation to the great general purpose for which the book was written, and the circumstances in which it was composed. To know that Paul wrote, at Ephesus, the first Epistle to the Corinthians, may help us to understand that third chapter in which the gold, silver, and precious stones of Diana's great fane are contrasted with the wood, hay, and stubble of the wretched huts and hovels of the abject poor. The Epistle *to the Hebrews* we shall expect to find full of references to Hebrew usages, customs, rites and ceremonies; and some things in it which would be stumbling-stones to gentile readers, become stepping-stones to the Hebrew believer.

We must not forget that every step of Biblical study should be pursued intelligently. We ought to go no faster and no farther than we understand. "Understandest thou what thou readest?" As in eating, it is not the quantity or even quality of food that determines nutritive value, but our power and capacity to appropriate and assimilate, so the profit of Bible study depends not on how much we read, but on how much we understand, receive, incorporate into ourselves. One verse thoroughly mastered, so that it lodges a new thought in the mind, a new joy in the heart, a new purpose in the life, is worth a hundred chapters read hastily, thoughtlessly, without leaving an impression behind. It pays to do thoroughly what we do at all, especially in Biblical study.

This book must be judged by its aim. It is the result of the author's search for keys to unlock the Word of God. Some key-word, with a corresponding key-text, being chosen as a general index to the contents of each book, the main features are sketched in bold outline, and minor details and divisions added in smaller type.

Before closing this introduction, we call our reader's attention to the *twelve conspicuous symbols* chosen in the Word of God, to represent its uses and the range and scope of its application to all our needs. We class them under seven divisions.

1. *The mirror*, to show us ourselves as we are and may be. (James i. 25.)

2. *The laver*, to wash away our sin and defilement. (Ephes. v. 26.)

3. The *lamp* and *light*, to guide us in the right way. (Ps. cxix. 105.)

4. The *milk, bread, strong meat,* and *honey*—affording sustenance and satisfaction to the believer, at all stages of spiritual development. (Hebrews v. 12-14; Ps. xix. 10, etc.)

5. The fine *gold*, to enrich us with heavenly treasure. (Ps. xix. 10.)

6. The *fire, hammer, sword*, to be used in the work and warfare of life. (Jer. xxiii. 29; Heb. iv. 12; Ephes. vi. 17.)

7. The *seed*, to beget souls in God's image and to plant harvest fields for God. (Jas. i. 18 1 Pet. i. 23; Matt. xiii.)

CONTENTS.

	PAGE
GENESIS	1
EXODUS	3
LEVITICUS	6
NUMBERS	9
DEUTERONOMY	12
JOSHUA	15
JUDGES	17
RUTH	19
I. II. SAMUEL	21
I. II. KINGS	24
I. II. CHRONICLES	27
EZRA, NEHEMIAH	31
ESTHER	35
THE POETIC BOOKS	37
JOB	41
PSALMS	43
PROVERBS	46
ECCLESIASTES	48
THE SONG OF SOLOMON	50

	PAGE
THE PROPHETS	53
ISAIAH	56
JEREMIAH	59
LAMENTATIONS	61
EZEKIEL	63
DANIEL	65
THE MINOR PROPHETS	68
HOSEA	71
JOEL	73
AMOS	74
OBADIAH	75
JONAH	76
MICAH	78
NAHUM	80
HABAKKUK	81
ZEPHANIAH	83
HAGGAI	85
ZECHARIAH	87
MALACHI	89
THE NEW TESTAMENT	92
THE FOUR GOSPELS	94
MATTHEW	96
MARK	98
LUKE	100
JOHN	102

	PAGE
ACTS	104
THE EPISTLES	106
ROMANS	107
I. CORINTHIANS	109
II. CORINTHIANS	111
GALATIANS	113
EPHESIANS	115
PHILIPPIANS	117
COLOSSIANS	119
I. II. THESSALONIANS	121
I. II. TIMOTHY	124
TITUS	127
PHILEMON	129
HEBREWS	132
JAMES	134
I. II. PETER	136
I. JOHN	138
II. JOHN	141
III. JOHN	142
JUDE	143
REVELATION	145

GENESIS.

Key-word: BEGINNING.   *Key-verse:* I.: 1.

THIS is the Book of the Beginnings. No beginning is ascribed to God, but all else had a beginning; and here, in direct statement or in illustration, suggestion, and type, all things, material or moral, are traced to their origin. Every great leading fact and truth, relation, and revelation are here found, the germs of all that is afterward more fully developed.

The beginnings are those of creation, the human race, marriage, the family, the State, the Church, nations, civilization, history; of law, penalty, government; of the Sabbath, sin, sacrifice, salvation; of worship, covenant, the call of God, the elect people; of promise and prophecy; of language, literature, mechanic arts, fine arts, science, and poetry.

The *primary truths* taught here are: the Unity, Trinity, eternity of the Godhead; God's natural attributes, power, wisdom, etc.; His moral attributes—holiness, goodness, etc.; the unity of the race, relation of husband and wife, of man to the animal creation, etc.

The *types of Christ: Adam*, married to **Eve**,

as Christ to the Church. *Sacrifice,* putting away sin and putting on righteousness, symbolized in the clothing of our first parents in the skins of slain beasts. *Abel,* the first martyr; *Noah,* preacher of righteousness; the *Ark;* *Melchizedek; Abraham; Isaac,* only son of promise, laid on the altar by his father and received back as from the dead; *Joseph,* from slavery and prison, raised to the throne, etc.

The Jews call this book by its first Hebrew word: the Greeks, " Genesis," — origination It is the oldest trustworthy book, and, without it, more than two thousand years would have no written history. Moses may have been guided by the Spirit to use material selected from earlier documents and traditions.

This book is the stately portal to the superb structure of the Holy Scripture. The opening sentence is a grand specimen of the beauty and truth, here compacted into the briefest compass. It excludes atheism, pantheism, polytheism, materialism; denies the eternity of matter, and teaches the eternity, self-existence, independence, omnipotence, and wisdom of the Creator.

DIVISIONS: I.: i.—xi. From Adam to Noah Sin, Fall, Deluge.

II.: xii.—l. Abraham to Joseph. The **Chosen Seed**; The Abode in Egypt; etc.

EXODUS.

Key-word: PASS-OVER.   *Key-verse:* XII. 23.

THIS is the book of the Exode or Departure. By a series of Ten Plagues, God delivers His elect nation from Bondage in Egypt. Blood now becomes the Sign and Pledge of Redemption. The word, Pass-over, has a threefold significance: God passed over the blood-sprinkled houses; then He caused to pass-over, or be set apart to Himself, all first-born (xiii. 12, margin); and He made Israel to pass-over the Red Sea, xv. 16.

The Ten Plagues are judgments against the gods of Egypt, xii. 12. The first and second against the idol river, the Nile. The third against the earth-god, Seb, and the priests who could not officiate with lice upon them. The fourth and eighth against Shu, the Atmosphere, son of Ra, the sun-god, against whom the ninth was directed. The fifth, against the Sacred Bull, Apis. The sixth, against Sutech or Typhon, the ashes of whose victims were flung to the winds. The seventh, against the Sacred Beetle, Scarabæus. The tenth, against all the gods at once, and the nation that decreed the wholesale destruction of the Hebrew children.

The central chapter is the *twelfth.* The Passover is a Pictorial Parable of Sin and Salvation. Its five marked features are: 1, Divine Judgment; 2, A life for a life; 3, Blood on the side and upper door-posts, but not on the threshold, where it would be trodden under foot, cf. Heb. x. 29; 4, God, passing over His people, when He saw the blood; 5, Consecration of all firstborn both of man and of beasts, and of firstfruits. Henceforth Redemption by blood and Peculiar Relation to the Redeemer become keys to the whole Word of God.

Here we have also the original "*Pilgrim's Progress*" begun. The *Pillar* of God's Presence leads the way, the Hiding of His Power, xiii. 21, 22. His *Tabernacle* is pitched among His People. Here He first makes known His name, *Jah*, "I am that I am," or "I am He who am" forever. Cf. John viii. 58; Heb. xiii. 8. His *Law* is graven upon stone to indicate its perpetual authority and force.

Moses is the central personage. His life divides into three periods, each of forty years: 1, From his Birth to his flight into Midian; 2, From his flight to the Exodus; 3, From the Exodus to his Death. His first attempt to deliver Israel failed, because it was in the power of the flesh; afterward he succeeded in the power of the spirit. He is a *type of Christ*, in the perils of his infancy, his voluntary surrender of royalty, his training in solitude, and his leadership of the people out of captivity.

DIVISIONS: I.: i.—xii. Israel in Egypt.
II.: xiii.—xviii. From Egypt to Sinai.
III.: xix.—xl. At Sinai; the Law given.

LEVITICUS.

Key-word: ATONEMENT. *Key-verse:* XVI. 34.

This is the Book of Worship, Sacrifice, and Priesthood. Exodus closes with God's Tabernacle in the midst of the tents of Israel. Leviticus opens with the Law of offerings. In order for the Holy One to dwell among sinners, and accept their service, there must be atonement by sacrifice and mediation by priesthood. The elect tribe, Levi, of the elect nation, represent the Appointed Days'-Man between God and men.

The central chapter is the *sixteenth*, and there is no more significant chapter in the Old Testament. On the *Great Day of Atonement*, the slain goat represents *guilt expiated by blood*, and the scape-goat, "azazel" or "removal," the *removal of offences* from before the face of God. Here is grace in its two aspects, *passing over* transgression and *remembering it no more.* **Cf.** Micah vii. 18, 19; Heb. viii. 12.

The *central personage* is Aaron, the High Priest; and the great themes of the book, acceptable approach, pardon and reconciliation and consecrated service.

The sacrifices or offerings are fivefold (i.–vii., xvi.): 1, The *Burnt-offering*, wholly consumed; 2, The *Meat* or food-offering, following the first, and bloodless because not expiatory; 3, *Peace-*offerings, slain but not wholly burned, part going to the Lord, part to the priest, and part back to the offerer; 4, *Sin-*offerings, strictly for atonement, and burned without the camp; 5, *Trespass-*offerings or Debt-offerings; where trespass was against the Lord, sacrifice preceded reparation; where it was against man, reparation preceded sacrifice. Cf. Matt. v. 23, 24. The first three were "*sweet-savour*" offerings, regarded not as consumed, but ascending in flame, like sweet incense to God. In the last two, which were *obligatory*, the offerer laid hands on the head of the victim, which was thus identified with his sin. All these offerings together typify Christ in His perfect offering of Himself for sin and unto God for service.

The Feasts are *eight*. Six are of days and months; two of years: 1, The *Sabbath;* 2, The *Passover* or unleavened bread; 3, *Pentecost* or the Feast of Weeks, fifty days or seven full weeks after the Passover; 4, *Trumpets*, on the first day of the seventh Lunar month; 5, *Atonement*, on the tenth of the seventh month; 6, *Tabernacles* or Booths, or Ingathering, five days later; 7, *Sabbatic year;* 8, *Jubilee* or fiftieth year, at the end of seven full heptades of years.

Here is a Sabbatic system: seventh day, week month, year, and heptade of years.

DIVISIONS: I.: i.—xvi. The Way to God by Sacrifice.

II.: xvii.—xxvii. The Walk with God by Sanctification and Separation.

NUMBERS.

Key-word: SOJOURN.   *Key-verse:* XXXIII. 1.

THIS is the Book of Pilgrimage and Service, the wilderness Wandering and Training. Two numberings of Israel are here recorded, representing organization, system, the Lord's Hosts equipped and marshalled for the march to Canaan. The time covered is about forty years, the beginning and end of the period being most prominent. Heb. iv. 1; Psalm xcv. 10, 11. Here we have Warfare as the necessary condition of Pilgrimage and Possession. God's worshippers are warriors. xxiii. 21.

The *central chapters* are the thirteenth and fourteenth. The tribes, at God's command, started from Sinai to possess the Promised Land, which was distant but eleven days' march. From Kadesh Barnea, on the borders of Canaan, twelve spies are sent ahead to explore the land. After forty days they return and report. The unbelieving Israel, afraid to trust God's word, murmur and rebel, and God condemns them to wander and sojourn in the wilderness for forty years, and all who had been numbered, save

Caleb and Joshua, the two faithful spies, to die there.

The backsliding nation lie *for the time under the ban.* In this chasm of thirty-eight years, Israel almost ceases to have, as God's people, a history. and all but their existence is engulfed. But one Passover is recorded as kept during all that time, and even circumcision was neglected. After this period, they are again at Kadesh Barnea, no nearer Canaan than before. So unbelief and disobedience always bring backsliding instead of progress, and believers have *no true history* as such, until they are renounced. All backsliders, before they make any advance, must come back to the point where rebellion began, and start anew.

The *numbering* may represent *God's appropriation of His own people;* He calleth them all by their names. Ps. cxlvii. 4; John x. 3, 4. It also represents the *organization* of the Lord's Host, both for *march* and for *war.* There were four divisions, each of three tribes. Whether moving or resting they formed a hollow square, within which was God's Tabernacle. If Tradition may be trusted, the central Tribal standards on each quarter were the *lion* (Judah), the *ox* (Ephraim), the *man* (Reuben), and the *eagle* (Dan). Cf. Psalm lxxx. 1, 2; Ezek. i. 10.

The *camp regulations* have reference to both *sanitation* and *sanctity.* The *marching* signals were both divine and human: the Cloud moving and the Trumpets sounding. *Miriam, Aaron,* and *Moses* all died before the passage of the Jordan: Prophecy, Priesthood, and Law, bring us to the borders; but only Jesus, our Joshua, leads us into our inheritance.

DIVISIONS: I.: i.—x. 10 Preparations for March from Sinai.

II.: x. 11.—xxi. Journey from Sinai to Moab.

III.: xxii.—xxxiv. In Moab preparing to enter Canaan.

DEUTERONOMY.

Key-word: OBEDIENCE. *Key-verse:* X. 12, 13.

THIS is the Book of the Second Law. As the first tables were broken and replaced, so the Law broken is made emphatic by repetition. The word, "remember," occurs some eighteen times, and the Deliverance from Egypt is constantly urged as a motive to *obedience.* Cf. v. 15. Israel, about to possess the Land, are reminded that this is the condition of entrance and continuance. Before Moses gives this new generation into Joshua's charge he rehearses the Moral Law.

The *central* chapter is the *twenty-ninth*, the covenant with God, where Moses in a few words condenses the argument of the whole book.

Four appeals to Israel make up the bulk of this book. *Seven principles* of obedience are set forth: 1, The Fatherhood of God and His Proprietorship in His People; 2, The duty of separation unto Him and His Service; 3, Worship to be localized and centralized; 4, All Idolatrous relics to be destroyed; 5, All Idolatrous acts to be treated as Treason against God, punished as capital crimes; 6, All ethical relations to be regulated by God's Law; 7, The Brotherhood of man implied in the Fatherhood of God.

This being the Book of Obedience, the words "*commandments,*" "*statutes,*" etc., are found here oftener than in any other book save the Psalms. The *Law* was to be *inscribed on Mt. Ebal*, the Mount of the Curse, for the end of the Law is condemnation. Such obedience as man can render secures *only temporal good;* hence among the blessings pronounced we do not find Eternal Life. Cf. xxviii. 1–13.

The *Prediction* about the *great coming Prophet*, xviii. 15–19, refers ultimately to Christ. Acts iii. 22, 23. He only acted as mediator, organizer, and administrator of the House of God; He only fulfils the prediction and the expectation which it inspires, and claims the implicit obedience here enjoined. It is noticeable that His three answers to Satan in the Temptation are all arrows drawn from this Book as a quiver. viii. 3; vi. 16; vi. 13.

Three Feasts are enjoined, chap. xvi. 1–17: The *Passover*, the *Pentecost* or *Feast of Weeks*, and the *Feast of Tabernacles*. The Passover is first, for the believer rests his Relationship with God upon Redemption by blood. Pentecost was the gathering of first-fruits, and the Feast of Tabernacles the Ingathering of the full Harvest. Together they typify a *completed Redemption:* first, by the Passion of the Cross; secondly, by the coming of the Holy Ghost; thirdly, by the Final Triumph of the Coming King; or suffering, grace, and glory.

This book is full of rich moral and spiritual lessons. The Law is recapitulated, enforced in the light of experience, both of mercy and judgment, not from the theoretical but from the practical side. xxx. 15, 16.

DIVISIONS: I.: i.—iv. Summary of Desert Wanderings.

II.: v. Rehearsal of the Decalogue.

III.: vi.—xxvi. Laws, etc., as to Conduct in Canaan.

IV.: xxvii.—xxviii. Blessings and Curses.

V.: xxix.—xxx. Covenant with God.

VI.: xxxi.—xxxii. Moses' Exhortation and "Song."

VII.: xxxiii. His Final "Blessing."

VIII.: Supplemental Narrative of Moses Death.

JOSHUA.

Key-word: POSSESSION.   *Key-verse:* I. 3.

THIS Book, which begins a new division of the Old Testament, is the book of *Entrance* and *Conquest, Possession* and *Dispossession.* The *Land of Promise* was larger than the *Land of Possession,* because God gave more than faith appropriated. Moses and the Law brought the Israelites to the borders of the inheritance into which Joshua, as the type of Jesus, leads. Even in the Promised Land there are conflicts. Possession is by Dispossession. Cf. Eph. vi. 10–18.

Joshua, being the *chief personage,* this book covers his career. Born in Egypt, of the tribe of Ephraim, he was captain at Rephidim, was with Moses in the Mount, like Caleb urged the people to go up and possess the Land, and died at 110 years of age, leaving a character without blemish. Moses appointed, the Lord anointed, him leader. Like Moses in zeal for God and love for Israel, he had more capacity and sagacity as a captain. The *Rod* was Moses' symbol; the *spear,* Joshua's.

The *crossing of Jordan* is by supernatural interposition. When the priests, bearing the ark, touch with their feet the overflowing river, the current is arrested; they stand in the river bed till all pass over; but as soon as they reach the farther bank the stream resumes its flow. The *two heaps* of stones are memorials; one of *Desert Pilgrimage*, the other of *Miraculous Passage*.

The *Reproach is rolled away* at Gilgal, and *Renewal of Covenant* prepares the people again to keep the *Passover*, and under the "Captain of the Lord's Host," to take the *typical stronghold, Jericho*, without striking a blow. *Defeat comes at Ai*, because of Achan's theft of "devoted" things; the entrance to the garden of the Land is with impressive ceremonies (viii. 30–35). The Tabernacle is set up at Shiloh, Cities of Refuge are appointed, and the Covenant of Separation ratified. Joshua's Death closes the Book.

Compare the *Book of Acts*, where Christ, by His Invisible Captain, the Spirit, conducts His church to Possession by Conquest; and heathen strongholds are taken, not by carnal weapons but by preaching and prayer.

DIVISIONS: I.: i.—xii. Conquest.
II.: xiii.—xxiv. Partition.

JUDGES.

Key-word: ANARCHY.   *Key-verse:* XXI. 25.

THIS Book is named from the *Period of Judges*, or civil and military chieftains between Joshua and Saul. Between 1500 and 1000 B.C. lay four or five centuries of disorganization and misgovernment. Idolatry and Conformity to the Age work ruin. Unity is lost; the tribes take the place of one People. Faith and faithfulness give way to unbelief and fickleness. The Tabernacle is hidden in darkness and there is but one mention of the High Priest. xx. 28.

There are *Fifteen Judges:* Othniel, Ehud, Shamgar, DEBORAH and Barak, Abimelech, GIDEON, Tola, Jair, Jephthah, Ibzan, Elon, Abdon, SAMSON, ELI, SAMUEL; the last, a prophet-judge, links the Judges and the Kings, as Deborah, a woman, is the prophet-judge linking Moses and Samuel. Samson, the Hercules of Scripture, is too weak to rule himself.

There are *Six Conquests:* by the Mesopotamians, Moabites, North Canaanites, Midianites, Ammonites, Philistines; and *Six* corresponding

Deliverances, under Othniel, Ehud, Deborah, Gideon, Jephthah, and Samson.

Joshua led into the Land of Promise, and gave Possession by Conquest. But unbelief and ungodliness forfeited further blessing and brought Decay to both Church and State. A picture of the whole period is in chapters xviii., xix. The author of this book is Samuel. (?)

History is full of Parallels. Micah and his Levite suggest the feudal castle and chieftain of the middle ages. The series of Captivities have their parallel in the Relapses of the Church into Pagan, Papal, and Pelagian errors, Ritualism, Rationalism, Secularism. From the Apostolic Age till now, extraordinary Deliverers have been raised up by God, such as Athanasius, Augustine, Chrysostom, Huss, Wycliffe, Luther, Knox, Bunyan, Wesley, Whitefield, Edwards, etc.

DIVISIONS: I.: i.—iii. 6. Introduction.
II.: iii. 7—xvi. Main History.
III.: xvii.—xxi. Appendix: fragmentary narratives without chronological order.

RUTH.

Key-word: KINSMAN (REDEEMER). *Key-verse:*
IV. 14.

THIS is a *Pastoral Idyl.* In Boaz, Redeemer (גֹּאֵל) of Ruth and her forfeited estate, two conditions must unite: he must be *kinsman* to have the *right;* and of a *higher branch* of the family, not involved in the disaster, to have the *power*, to redeem. The Race is in ruin. Man is next of kin, but cannot redeem his fellow-man, for he is ruined himself. The God-man, our near kinsman, yet of a higher family, becomes both Redeemer and Bridegroom of the Church.

This *Sacred Love Story* has a typical aspect. Famine in Bethlehem (House of Bread), drives Elimelech (God, my King) to Moab, Land of Aliens. There, amid altars of Chemosh (vanquishing foe?) he dies, and after him his sons Mahlon (song), and Chilion (Perfection), leaving Moabite widows, Orpah (skull?) and Ruth (Satisfied). Ten years later, Naomi (sweet?) returns with Ruth. Guided by Providence, she gleans in the fields of Boaz (in Him strength). He looks on her with favor, buys back her estate and marries her. The Moabite, shut out by Law (Deut. xxiii. 3), is admitted by grace, not only to the congregation of the Lord, but to the ancestral line of Messiah, who, like Boaz, is Lord of Harvest, Dispenser of Bread, Giver of Rest.

Even *Lack of Bread* does not warrant departure from God and identification with the forbidden land of Aliens. Calamity follows disobedience; the backslider must return from alienation and separation, and be reunited to the Lord and His people, before prosperity returns. Orpah represents the sinner rejecting; Ruth, the sinner repenting, believing, coming to the Redeemer, poor and friendless, lying at His feet, praying for the shelter of His name, the protection and provision of His love, the participation of His life and bliss, and finding in Him more than hope dared anticipate. Ruth is the forerunner of the Gentiles incorporated into the Church.

I. II. SAMUEL.

Key-word: KINGDOM. *Key-verse:* I. SAM. X. 25

THESE two books form one in the Hebrew, and in old English versions made, with the two following, Four Books of Kings. The history covers about 120 years and moves mainly about *Samuel, Saul,* and *David.* The prominent, dominant idea is *the Kingdom:* its matter, manner, renewal, and rending; its translation from Saul the Apostate, its deliverance from Absalom the Usurper, and its establishment in the hands of David. The name "Messiah" is first found here. 1 Sam. ii. 10 (Hebrew).

Samuel was born when anarchy reigned. Eli, high-priest and judge, was too old and weak to curb even his own vile sons. This child, "asked of God," and while serving at the Tabernacle in Shiloh, heard from God the doom of Eli's house; and in him prophetic open visions were revived. A judge as well as a seer, he emphasized *obedience* more than *offerings.* In old age he could challenge all Israel to find in him one breach of piety or probity; but his sons were unfit to succeed him. Hence the clamor for a king; the prayer was not of faith; God gave their request, but sent leanness to their souls.

Saul, the first king, was of fine person, and his mingled merit and modesty won even opponents; but two years later apostasy began. His folly at Gilgal, and his falsehood and rebellion in the war with Amalek, led to his *Rejection*. His decline was rapid, possessed by an evil demon, and enslaved by bad passions. He hunted David like a bird, and sought to slay his own son. Forsaken by God, he sought at Endor one of the witches he had driven from the land; an apparition of Samuel warned him of his speedy death, and he fell the next day by his own hand.

David, his successor, was *thrice anointed:* first at Bethlehem, privately; then at Hebron, over Judah; then over all Israel. Before taking the kingdom, he slew Goliath, the Philistine giant, and became the bosom friend of Jonathan.

II. Samuel opens with *David's Lament* over Saul and Jonathan. Abner, Saul's captain, proclaimed Ishbosheth, son of Saul, king, and for seven and a half years David's reign was limited to Judah; then Abner went over to David's side and was slain by Joab, and Ishbosheth was assassinated. David was by common consent made king over all Israel, with his capital at Jerusalem.

The narrative abounds in suggestions. **Poet.**

ic retribution finds examples in Saul's history; also in David's, whose great sin brought correct-ive punishment in its own line, in the death of the child of his crime, and the incest of Amnon and Absalom. *Implicit obedience* is enforced. David's attempt to bring up the Ark *on a cart* issued in the death of Uzzah; three months later he had it borne *on the shoulders of the Levites*, as God had directed. *Godly Repentance* is illustrated. The guilt of adultery, treachery, and murder lay heavy on David. Nathan's parable of the ewe-lamb touched the spring of godly sorrow which overflows in Psalm li. *Grace* finds illustration in David's treatment of Absalom and Mephibosheth, and in the Arrested Judgment at Araunah's threshing-floor, which became the site of the Temple with its Altar of Atonement.

DIVISIONS: I.: I. Sam. i.—vii. Samuel, the Prophet-Judge.

II.: I. Sam. viii.—xxxi. Saul's Career.

III.: II. Sam. i.—v. 5. David, King over Judah.

V.: II. Sam. v. 6—xx. David, King over Israel.

VI.: II Sam. xxi.—**xxiv. Appendix.**

I. II. KINGS.

Key-word: ROYALTY. *Key-verse:* I. KINGS II 12; XI. 13.

THESE two books, which again form one in the original, follow the monarchy from its highest glory, through decline and division to final downfall. Under Solomon, Royalty rises to the summit of its splendor, with the Temple as its crown. Extravagant outlay and display, heathen wives and idol fanes, bring the kingdom to wreck, and each of the divisions ends in captivity and dispersion. Author, Jeremiah. (?)

Adonijah's attempted usurpation opens the first book, followed by the coronation of Solomon, and the deaths of the usurper, of Joab and Shimei, the deposition of Abiathar the Priest, and the establishment of the kingdom in Solomon's hand.

Solomon's *divine Gift of Wisdom* seems to have been a rare blending of mental capacity and moral sagacity. To large endowments he added large acquirements in natural and moral science. Sages, like the Queen of Sheba, journeyed from afar to hear his discourse, and found the facts to exceed even his fame. His Proverbs are marvels of common sense and practical wisdom.

Excessive outlay marked his reign. To the Temple which rose on Moriah like a shrine of alabaster and gold, he added a Palace with an ivory throne, and other costly structures; and the cities, pools, and public works which he built outshone any others of his day. He made alliances with foreign courts, and kept a vast harem. All this worldly splendor implied heavy costs and imposed heavy taxes; popular murmurs forecast the wreck of the kingdom under Rehoboam. *Judah*, partially supported by Simeon and Benjamin, remained loyal to David's House; the other tribes, confederate under Jeroboam, made Shechem their capital, and *calves* were set up at Dan and Bethel to keep the people from going to worship at Jerusalem.

Elijah and Elisha, the two remarkable prophets which appear in the Northern Kingdom, are strange counterparts. *Elijah* suddenly appears, a full-grown seer, facing Ahab with flaming reproof. A supernatural atmosphere is about him. He is fed and kept by miracle; his prayers command the rains and fires of heaven, to which at last he rides in a chariot of fire; the only man, beside Enoch, ever translated. He is like a lion, strong, stern; a child of the desert, living in the caves of Horeb, the ciefts of Cherith, or the cliffs of Carmel. He enters the city with fiery rebuke, and departs again into ascetic solitude. He is dressed in a rough robe, and comes as a destroyer of idols.

Elisha is his complement; like a lamb, gentle, humble; he dwells in cities, is urbane and courteous, mingles with the sons of the prophets and the elders. He wears an ordinary garment and bears a staff; he is tolerant and benignant, and comes as a healer and helper. Even the *names Elijah* (Jehovah my God), and *Elisha* (Jehovah my Saviour), suggest appositeness. One may represent *Law;* the other, *Grace.*

This history shows the ruin to which a *False Liberalism* leads. Solomon's polygamy and pagan wives led him first to forbear with heathen rites, and then to build fanes for false gods over against Jehovah's Temple. This, and the *calf-worship* which broke the *second* commandment, paved the way for the *Baal-worship* under Ahab and Jezebel which broke the *first.*

DIVISIONS: I.: I. Kings i.—xi. From Solomon's Coronation to Death.

II.: I. Kings xii.—II. Kings xvii. From Rehoboam to the Captivity of Israel under the Assyrians.

III.: II. Kings xviii.—xxv. From Hezekiah to the Captivity of Judah under the Chaldeans.

I. II. CHRONICLES.

Key-word: THEOCRACY. *Key-verse:* II. CHRON XV. 2.

THESE two books, one in the original, close the Hebrew Canon. Their purpose is more than mere historical repetition or completion. Their ruling idea is *theocratic.* Human kingdoms must represent God-Rule. Only while He is recognized and reverenced; only as Temple worship is neither neglected nor corrupted, can there be true prosperity.

"Chronicles" means "Words of Days," Journals: the Septuagint title is, "Things Omitted" or "Supplementary" ($\pi\alpha\rho\alpha\lambda\epsilon\iota\pi\omicron\mu\epsilon\nu\alpha$). But neither name expresses or exhausts the purpose and purport of these books. The people, now returned from captivity, have rebuilt the Temple, but not the fabric of their nationality. Ezra was probably the author, and he seeks upon *Judah as a basis* to reconstruct a consecrated nation. This priestly scribe traces the Redemption line from Adam to David, and thence to Judah's last king. The Division of Families and possessions, and the Levitical courses as before the Captivity, are recorded with a view to restoration.

While much contained in the Books of Kings is repeated or restated, much is omitted because foreign to the author's purpose. But whatever bears on the Temple, its preservation and restoration, the purity of its worship, the regularity and orderliness of its services; whatever makes idolatrous rites or relics hateful, or lifts God to His true throne in the hearts of the people, is here emphasized. *The attitude of the kings toward the King of kings* is shown to be the key of national History, with its rewards or penalties. The fall of the Temple and the long exile are shown to have followed upon a succession of three wicked and idolatrous kings, while every true Reformer of national character and Religious worship is held up as one who has stayed the plague.

This purpose being seen, it is easy to account both for the likeness and unlikeness of the Books of Kings and of Chronicles. The *former* concern *both kingdoms*, and are political and kingly, the *latter* concern *Judah* only, and are ecclesiastical and priestly. One, as a record of history, *annalizes;* the other, as a philosophy of history, *analyzes*. In "Kings" we find wars, idolatries, offences; in Chronicles, deliverances, repentance, reformation. In one, idolatry is treason against the Supreme King; in the other, apostasy from the Covenant God. Cf. II. Kings xvii. 7–23; II. Chron. xxxvi. 14–21.

The Temple is naturally in the foreground. David's preparations for the building, in the first book; Solomon's erection and dedication of it, in the second. The splendid structure, sanctified *to* God's glory, was sanctified *by* God's glory. Those of Solomon's successors who jealously and zealously guarded the Holy House, have a special memorial here: Asa, who deposed the Queen Dowager, his own mother, for indirectly profaning it by her idol grove; Joash, Hezekiah, and Josiah, who repaired it and led in the renewal of covenant and destruction of idols.

The *Service of Song* in the House of the Lord, is fully set forth, as conducted by two hundred and eighty-eight trained singers and players, with a chorus of four thousand, led by Asaph, Heman, and Jeduthun. It was only a monotonous chant in unison, with no intricacies of time or harmony, varied by responsive choirs, with great volume of voice and instrumental accompaniment. Its aim was not *art*, but *worship*, in sharp contrast with the modern perversions of "sacred song."

Four deliverances are here recorded as wrought for Judah: under Abijah, against Jeroboam; under Asa, against the Ethiopians; under Jehoshaphat, against the Moabites: and under

Hezekiah, against the Assyrians. And in every instance success is attributed to *God's fighting for Judah.* II. Chron. xiii. 18; xiv. 11; xx. 27; xxxii. 21, 22.

DIVISIONS: I.: I. Chron. i.—ix. Genealogies, etc.

II.: I. Chron. x.—xxix. Kingdom under David.

III.: II. Chron. i.—ix. Kingdom under Solomon.

IV.: II. Chron. x.—xxxvi. Kingdom from Rehoboam to Zedekiah.

EZRA. NEHEMIAH.

Key-word: RESTORATION. *Key-verse:* **EZRA** I. 5; NEH. II. 5.

THESE two are companion books, regarded by the Hebrews as one. Both treat of the Return from Babylon and the Restoration and Reorganization: the former of ecclesiastical history and the rebuilding of the Temple under Ezra; the latter of civil history and the rebuilding of the city under Nehemiah. Together, they present a complete picture of post-captivity reconstruction and reorganization in Church and State.

Ezra, probable author of the book bearing his name, was an Aaronic priest, scribe, and the compiler of the Old Testament canon. This book, like Chronicles, contains genealogical lists; it covers about eighty years, and in its record four Gentile kings appear: Cyrus, Darius, Ahasuerus, Artaxerxes.

Fifty thousand captives returned under lead of Zerubbabel, called by the Persians, Sheshbazzar, and Jeshua or Joshua, High Priest. This colony, to whom Cyrus gave in charge the sacred vessels stolen from the Lord's House, laid the foundations of the second Temple. Samaritans and other half-pagan colonists whose help was refused, prejudiced the Persian Power, and stopped the work. After long delay, the people, stirred up by Haggai and Zechariah, appealed to the original decree of Cyrus, which was found and confirmed by Darius; and after twenty years the work was completed.

The prophetic *seventy years* of Captivity may be reckoned either from the Destruction of the First Temple to the Dedication of the Second, 588–518 B.C.; or from the First Invasion of Nebuchadnezzar to the Decree of Cyrus, 606–536 B.C. The Jews were cured of idolatry by experience in exile, but were entangled in pagan alliances. Ezra, leading in confession and reformation, annulled mixed marriages and revived the knowledge and authority of the Law. About sixty years after the first colony, a second left Babylon under Ezra, and about thirteen years later, a third under Nehemiah.

Nehemiah, born in exile, became cup-bearer to the king. By royal grant, and with letters of authority, he went to rebuild Jerusalem. He found the city in partial ruin and the people in partial indifference. Beginning every work with prayer and fasting, he surveyed the walls by night, and then urged the leaders to rebuild. Though opposed by Arabian, Ammonite, and Moabite, he pushed on the work, enlisting all classes, from the High Priest down to the women.

Nehemiah, the *Model Organizer*, proved the worth of method and system. His *five principles* were: 1, Division of Labor; 2, Adaptation of Work and Worker; 3, Honesty and Economy in Administration; 4, Co-operation in labor; 5, Concentration at any assaulted point.

His *character is without blot.* He was a man of faith, bold, resolute, energetic, with peculiar prayerfulness and reserve power. He stood like an anvil, till the hammers of opposition wore themselves out vainly beating against him.

His *Work of Restoration* began at the *sheep-gate*, through which victims were led to the altar. Rebuilding was followed by Reforming: as Governor he corrected the abuses of the rich and the oppression of the poor, revived the knowledge of God's Law, Sabbath observance, free-will offerings and covenant obligations. His return to Persia was followed by decline of morals; but he came back to the Holy City, purged the Temple courts, and again purified the family and the State.

DIVISIONS: *Ezra.* I.: i.—vi. Return from Captivity, etc.

II.: vii.—x. Events in reign of Artaxerxes, etc.

Between these two sections lies a gap of fifty-seven years.

Nehemiah. I.: i.—vii. Nehemiah's narrative.

II. : viii.—ix. Narrative continued by another party.

III.: xi.—xii. 26. Six important lists.

IV.: xii. 27—xiii. Dedication of Wall and Reforms.

ESTHER.

Key-word: PROVIDENCE. *Key-verse:* IV. 14.

THIS book is the *Romance* of *Providence*. Esther, a Jewish captive, became bride of the Persian king, Ahasuerus; and came to the kingdom for a critical time. Haman's wicked plot to destroy her people, baffled by her bold intercession, reacted to his own ruin. The Feast of Purim (the Lot), instituted by the Jews in memory of this Deliverance, is still kept. As Ruth represents the Gentiles coming to the church, Esther illustrates the church going to the Gentiles.

The *Doctrine of God's Providence* finds here a historic pictorial parable. 1. There is behind human affairs an Unseen Hand. 2. Both evil and good have their ultimate awards. 3. The prosperity of the wicked is unsafe and unsatisfying, ending in adversity. 4. The adversity of the good is a trial of faith, issuing in prosperity. 5. Retribution is administered with poetic exactness. 6. The most minute events are woven into God's plan. 7. Providence is not Fate, but consists with Prayer and Resolve, Freedom and Responsibility.

The *Name of God* is not found here. His is a *Secret Control* of the affairs of His People: a *Hidden Hand* shifts the scenes. Only the Eye of Faith sees the Divine Factor in human history, but to the attentive observer all history is a Burning Bush aflame with the mysterious Presence. This book is the rose window in the cathedral structure of the Old Testament. If the light it transmits be dim, it reveals exquisite tracery and symbolic design in the framework and colored panes.

Grace is here illustrated. There is substitution, voluntary and vicarious sacrifice, a sceptre extended to a suppliant, audience with the king and answered prayer; promises without limit (viii. 8), and final victory over all foes.

THE POETIC BOOKS

THE Old Testament was popularly divided into the "Law," "Prophets," and "Psalms," Luke xxiv. 44. The "Psalms" include five poetical books, from Job to Solomon's Song inclusive.

The *Genius of Hebrew Poetry* is peculiar. It does not depend on rhyme or rhythm, metre or melody, but on *Parallelism*, or the arrangement of thought in corresponding or parallel sentences and stanzas. The poetry lies rather in the relation of the thoughts than the words; there is a rhyme and rhythm of ideas.

A wonderful provision is thus made *for translation*. This parallelism of thought can be reproduced in any language without any necessary loss of its beauty or power in the transfer from one tongue to another.

Parallelism is of five kinds: Apposite, Opposite, Synonymous, Synthetic, Inverted.

1. *Apposite:* where two or more parallel sentences are arranged so as to present the same or closely related thoughts, by way of correspondence or comparison. Thus Proverbs iii. 5:

"Trust in the Lord with all thine heart;
And lean not unto thine own understanding."

Here the one thought, *trusting in Jehovah*, is presented in both members, first positively, then negatively. The truly wise man trusts in God, and does not trust in himself.

2. *Opposite*: where exactly opposite thoughts are contrasted, with sharp antithesis. Thus Proverbs x. 7:

"The memory of the just is blessed;
But the name of the wicked shall rot.'

Here the antithesis extends to all the prominent words of both members.

3. *Synonymous*: where the same thought is repeated in equivalent terms and phrases. Thus Proverbs i. 4:

"To give subtilty to the simple;
To the young man, knowledge and discretion."

4. *Synthetic*: where thoughts are built up into structural form, like block upon block, cumulatively and often climacterically. Before the whole idea is complete, several successive pairs of parallels may enter into the construction. Thus Proverbs xxx. 17:

"The eye that mocketh at his father,
And despiseth to obey his mother:
The ravens of the valley shall pick it out,
And the young eagles (vultures) shall eat it."

Here are two synonymous parallels built up into one synthetic. Agur's Prayer, Prov. xxx. 7–9, and the passage from verses 24–28, are examples of still more complex synthetic parallelism. Some are very complicated; the correspondence between the various propositions reaches even to minor details; and the whole paragraph with its constructive parts crystallizes about one dominant idea. Cf. Psalm cxlviii. 7–13; xix. 7–11.

5. *Inverted:* where stanzas are so framed that, to perceive the true relations of the sentences we must begin at the extremes and move toward the centre. Bishop Jebb calls this "Introverted." Thus Psalm cxxxv. 15–18:

> " The idols of the heathen are silver and gold,
>   The work of men's hand;
>   They have mouths, but they speak not;
>   They have eyes, but they see not;
>   They have ears, but they hear not;
>   Neither is there any breath in their mouths.
>   They who make them are like unto them;
> So are all they who put their trust in them."

The relation of the various lines and members will appear from the above arrangement, where correspondent clauses are placed directly opposite each other.

To master this symmetric structure of poetic parts of the Bible is a help to intelligent *exposition* and *exegesis*. The mutual relation of the words and thoughts will not appear until we discover what phrases or sentences are parallel, and detect the thought-rhythm. Thus Psalm x. 4, translating literally:

> "The wicked in the height of his scorn:
>   'He will not require it!'
>   'There is no God!'
> *These are* all his thoughts."

Here the wicked is represented at the very apex and climax of daring impiety and blasphemy. His secret thought is: "God will not requite my sin," and from this denial of judgment the step is easy to the last and worst thought: "There is no God!"

Once more. Matthew vii. 6:

> "Give not that which is holy unto the dogs;
>   Neither cast ye your pearls before swine,
>   Lest they trample them under their feet,
> And turn again and rend you."

At first glance, all the latter half of this stanza would be referred to the swine. But every part of such a stanza demands its parallel, and the law of thought-rhyme leads us to construe the last line as the correspondent and complement of the first.

> "Give not that which is holy unto the dogs,
>   Lest they turn again and rend you;
>   Neither cast ye your pearls before swine,
> Lest they trample them under their feet."

JOB.

Key-word: TRIAL. *Key-verse:* I. 9.

This Book solves a problem. Satan asks: "Doth Job serve God for naught?" This oriental tale is the answer: Uprightness may survive the loss of all temporal good. Disaster to property and family, and disease in his own person, together, could not bring Job to curse God whom he feared, nor to do the evil which he hated. Subordinately, another problem is here discussed: the uses of adversity.

Job's trial is a test of his trust in God, and of the truth of his life. The sorest sufferings will not lead a true saint to forsake God or Godliness. This man, though morally and religiously upright, is suddenly struck down: the blow falls on his possessions, his household, himself; he is smitten with that supposed "scourge of God" and brand of His curse, Elephantiasis (?). In return he is tempted to curse God: 1, By the perplexity which such calamities cause to the consciously upright; 2, By the continuation, accumulation, and aggravation of his trials; 3, By the remonstrance of his instinct of natural justice; 4, By the charges of guilt and hypocrisy;

5, By the hateful taunts of his own wife. But he holds fast his integrity because he loves goodness for its own sake, irrespective of reward.

Job's three friends seek to solve that other problem of the Divine Government: the *Philosophy of suffering*. They discuss it in the light of History, Philosophy, and Natural Law; but even Elihu, with his deeper insight, only presents half-truths. Then God speaks, correcting errors and completing truths: the mystery of Trial is explained. Suffering finds its philosophy, not in *organic penalty* and *retributive judgment* only, but also in *disciplinary chastisement* and *educative development*.

This Book suggests a *key to the whole Bible*, and *to man's history* from creation to completed Redemption. 1, Man unfallen and untried; 2, Sinning and suffering; 3, Seeking human help in legality, morality, philosophy; 4, Needing and receiving a Revelation from God; 5, Humbled, penitent, believing; 6, Restored to a better estate than at first.

The *scene of the book* is laid in the Patriarchal era, between chapters xi. and xii. of Genesis (?). The author, probably Elihu. Cf. xxxii. 15-17.

DIVISIONS: I.: i.—ii. Historical Prologue.

II.: iii.—xlii. 6. Allegorical narrative with semi-dramatic dialogue and tripartite division.

III.: xlii. 7-17. Historical Epilogue.

PSALMS.

Key-word: WORSHIP.   *Key-verse:* XXIX. 2.

THE Psalter is a Book of Devotion for the Ages. Here every heart-chord is touched and tuned to holy melody. God is here in His natural and moral attributes. Christ is here in His divinity and humanity, humiliation and exaltation. The Gospel is here: sublime unfoldings of pardoning and purifying grace. Christian life is here, faith hope, love; and even church history in outline.

This is *a collection of one hundred and fifty lyrics* for public and private worship. The Greek title, "Psalms," means songs set to music; the Hebrew title is "Praises," which make up the bulk of the book, and breathe in almost every psalm; with praise the book begins and ends; and into praise, penitence and prayer and perplexity at last merge and melt. Praise ranges over Creation, Providence, and Grace; abounding more as we advance the farther, till the climax is reached in the Hallelujah Psalms.

The authors and eras are not the same. One-third are anonymous; seventy-three are by

David; twelve ascribed to Asaph; eleven to the sons of Korah; two to Solomon; one to Moses, etc. The *eras* reach from the Desert Wanderings to the Return from Captivity, the older Psalms generally preceding. The *Inscriptions* should be studied; they show which are Songs of Love, Pilgrimage, or Memorial, and whether meant for praise, prayer, or instruction.

Here are *Pearls*, precious and plentiful The first three Psalms are *keys to the entire collection;* their themes are the Scriptures, the Messiah, and the believers' experience: xiv. and liii. are virtually the same; xix. and cxix. are monuments to God's Law; xxii. xxiii. xxiv. correspond respectively to Messiah's Passion and Crucifixion, Death and Burial, Resurrection and Ascension; xlv., the Canticle-Psalm, is a key to Solomon's Song; li. is the Psalm of Penitence; xxxii. of Pardon; xlv. of Salvation; xlvi. of Faith: xxxvii. of Assurance; l. of Sacrifice; lxxii. of Missions; lxxiii. is the Sceptic's Psalm; lxxxv. the Beggar's Psalm; xc. xci. the Psalms of Death and of Life; cvi. cvii. of Ingratitude, and of Gratitude; cxiii.–cxviii. Hallelujah Psalms; cxx.–cxxxiii. Psalms of Ascents, sung when going up to Temple Feasts.

Believers have always regarded the Psalter as a precious heritage. Athanasius called it "an Epitome of all Scripture"; Luther, ' a little Bible"; Basil, "the Common Treasure of all good precepts"; and Bishop Alexander has traced therein a wonderful "Witness to Christ and Christianity."

DIVISIONS: Five books, marked by their peculiar endings:

I.: i.—xli. Ending with Doxology and double Amen.

II.: xlii.—lxxii. Same ending, with the sentence: "The Prayers of David . . . . are ended."

III.: lxxiii.—lxxxix. Same ending as Book I.

IV.: xc.—cvi. Same, with Hallelujah.

V.: cvii.—cl. Ending with many Hallelujahs.

PROVERBS.

Key-word: WISDOM. *Key-verse:* IX. 10.

HERE is exhibited wisdom in practical life, shaping character and conduct, regulating alike man's relations to man and to God. True wisdom develops manhood, leads to morality, and in its highest reach, to piety; it demands obedience to both Tables of the Law. It makes the understanding clear, the heart clean, the conscience pure, and the will firm. Wisdom as here personified, corresponds to the Word, or Logos, in John.

The *word, rendered "Proverb,"* means Parable or authoritative saying, and hints that moral truths are taught by comparison or contrast. The English word, Proverb, means a brief saying in the stead of many words (*pro-verba*), and implies *pithiness in parallelism*. Proverbs have always been the mottoes that mould life and history. The *power of a Proverb* lies partly in its *form;* it is short, sharp, incisive, impressive. It assumes truth, attracts attention, and imprints itself on the memory. The Hebrew

Proverbs, 'like forceps," hold truth firmly between the opposing points of antithesis.

This Book is a *compilation.* Many of these Proverbs are of earlier date, and some are acknowledged to be the "Words of Agur," "Lemuel," etc.; but Solomon's sayings make up the bulk of the book (I. Kings iv. 32). His gift of wisdom finds expression in wise and witty apothegms, that show his intellectual capacity and moral sagacity, his habits of close observation and scientific thought, his common sense and uncommon knowledge of human nature. The subjects treated are such as filial piety, evil company, sensuality and drunkenness, lying and laziness, strife and greed. Chapter xxxi. contains a fine acrostic on the "virtuous woman." What the Psalms are to devotional life, the Proverbs are to practical life.

DIVISIONS: I.: i.—ix. Admonitions especially to the Young.

II.: x.—xxiv. Miscellaneous, for all classes.

III.: xxv.—xxix. Later Collections by Scribes under Hezekiah, etc.

IV.: xxx. xxxi. Supplement. Words of Agur and Lemuel.

ECCLESIASTES.

Key-word: VANITY.   *Key-verse:* II. 11.

THESE "Words of the Preacher," in a sort of monologue, record results of experience and observation as to the Life of Man. Looked at from the loftiest level "*under the sun,*" all seems a dismal failure, " vanity and vexation." Only when this world and the world to come are joined, do we get the *whole of life;* only when God and man are joined by faith and obedience do we get the *whole of man.* See xii. 13, 14.

Ecclesiastes is an enigma to many readers who see in Solomon an epicure, dyspeptic, hypochondriac, or sceptic. To a closer student the plan of the book becomes plain. As seen *from this world only, Life is not worth living,* and the preface anticipates and outlines the argument: 1. *Death ends all* in defeat and disappointment. 2. *All moves in an endless circle* of monotonous repetition, nothing new, no permanent progress. 3. *All labor fails to satisfy or gratify.* 4. *All is lost at last,* even the remembrance of good.

After this prefatory outline he *enters into detail.* He follows a scientific method, gathering facts, classifying them, and drawing inferences and inductions. His *experiments* are: pursuit of wisdom, pleasure, frivolity, worldly enterprise, treasure, and the fine arts; but he only reaches the climax of disgust. ii. 26. His *observations* are: man is limited by a law of Destiny; and vanity and vexation are the two words that express his final verdict.

The *Solution of this Problem* of Life begins at chapter viii. 16. He finds: 1, A Divine Providence ruling all; 2, Pious remembrance of God introducing into life a saving factor, that turns vanity into verity, and vexation into satisfaction; 3, This world is a hemisphere, whose complement is another; man is a half-hinge without God. Under the sun there is no profit, but we must look beyond the sun. "Fear God and keep His Commandments; for this is the WHOLE OF MAN." xii. 13, 14.

DIVISIONS: I.: i. 1–11. Preface.
II.: i. 12—ii. 26. Results of Experiment.
III.: iii.—viii. 15. Results of Observation
IV.: Induction. viii. 16—xii. 7.
V.: Grand Conclusion. xii. 8–14

THE SONG OF SOLOMON

Key-word: BELOVED.   *Key-verse:* VI. 3.

IN this Epithalamium, or Marriage-Song by a dialogue between Bridegroom and Bride the mystery of Christ and His Church appears to be typified. Cf. Eph. v. 25-32. The Forty-fifth Psalm, "A Song of Loves," briefly treats the same theme in the same way, and is a key to Canticles. The marriage-bond is the favorite figure whereby both prophets and apostles represent Jehovah's relation to His People. Cf. Isa. lxii. 5; Jer. iii.; Ezek. xvi.

The *parties in this nuptial dialogue*, or antiphonal chant, are *Shelomoh*, Prince of Peace, and *Shulamith*, Seeker of Peace; names that correspond as do Julius and Julia, or Francis and Frances. Shulamith is not only *feminine*, but *collective*, for the Church is a collective body; hence the frequent use of the plural "*we*," as in i. 4. Though black with exposure to a tropical sun, she is comely in his eyes who calls her his "Love." She was made for him, and her heart is as restless as a wandering dove, till it rests in Him.

Transitions in the dialogue are traced by change of pronouns, and by the sense. The typical interpretation is the only natural and satisfactory one. Wedded Love is the type of the peculiarly affectionate, intimate, confidential, and exclusive union between Christ and believers. The Bride's constant thought and praise of the Bridegroom suggest the devotion of the disciple to his Lord, while the Bridegroom's tender love to her suggests the Lord's unspeakable grace, who loved the Church and gave Himself for her, who sanctifies and cleanses her, nourishes and cherishes her, and, finally, presents her to Himself. A close study may find in this poem the *successive stages* of the believer's growth in knowledge, love, and joy, from the first taste of delight in Jesus, in the reconciling kiss, to the crowning ecstasy found in the consciousness that He delights in the disciple.

The order and succession of these two books is suggestive. In Ecclesiastes, man finds his soul too great for this world to feed and fill: all is vanity; there is no profit under the sun. In Canticles, man, looking above the sun, finds in God what not only fills his soul, but cannot be contained. The sea fills the cup, but the cup does not hold the sea. And so from *vanity* we come to *verity*.

It will be found helpful to disregard the old divisions of chapters, and divide this dialogue into six sections, beginning respectively at chaps. i. 2, ii. 7, iii. 6, v. 2, vi. 10, and viii. 5.

DIVISIONS: I.: i. 1. Inscription.

II.: i. 2—v. 1. The Bride in the King's Chamber; His Visit, Her Dream, and the Royal Espousals.

III.: v. 2—viii. 14. The King's Wife; Seeking and Finding; The Return Home, etc.

THE PROPHETS.

HERE begins the third and last division of the Old Testament. A prophet is not necessarily one who predicts, but one who *speaks for God*, an inspired teacher. Prediction was one form in which the divine seal and sanction were set upon the prophet. The prophetic and historic books are closely related. The *Hebrew nation is always the centre of both*, and other nations are viewed only as related to this central subject and object.

There are *seventeen prophetic* books: five belong to the *major*, and twelve to the *minor* prophets: but these terms refer to length, not to comparative importance. They are not in chronological order: four or five of the minor prophets antedate Isaiah. The period covered by these books spans over four centuries, from about 870 to 440 B.C., and is marked by three divisions: *Pre-Exile*, *Exile*, and *Post-Exile*. It is of great importance to study the prophecies with relation to the period which they cover, as the history will often interpret the prophecy.

The Hebrew is the central figure in prophecy;

first in the *national* or organic aspect; secondly in the *ecclesiastical,* or *spiritual,* with reference to the believing remnant; and thirdly, in the *personal,* or Messianic. These are so intermingled as often to be indistinguishable. Predictions relate either to Judah, or Israel, or the nations by whom they were oppressed. Whatever judgments are foretold, a promise of restoration relieves the darkness; the believing Remnant survives to become a blessing to all people.

Two expressions abound in prophecy: "The Last Days," and "The Day of the Lord." The first covers all that series of events associated with the period bounded by our Lord's First Advent and by the Final Judgment. The Day of the Lord is the dark aspect of Judgment seen in connection with those Last Days, and marks the crisis and catastrophe.

Some *principles of interpretation* should be observed. Prophecy often presents at first an outline or profile of coming events, which successive prophecies fill out and complete; so that only by combination and comparison the whole picture is seen. Again, prophetic perspective often foreshortens the future. Events are seen in outline, and in series or succession, without regard to intervals between, or comparative proportions or dimensions. One outline may correspond to different events; a prediction, apparently fulfilled, may still await a grander accomplishment. Later prophecies will often be found to expand previous predictions, and analyze and separate what was before vague, confused, and general. The horizon enlarges as it is approached.

The *Key to all prophecy* is *The Kingdom of God;* its Rise, Progress, Conflicts, and Final Triumph; from First to Last, however various its aspects, in essence and principle one **and unchangeable.**

ISAIAH.

Key-word: SALVATION. *Key-verse:* LIII. 5.

THE Testimony of Jesus is the spirit of Prophecy. This is the Song of Christ tracing the great facts and features of His life and work, from His cradle to His crown. The Heart of the Old Testament is the Fifty-third Chapter, where God's Suffering Servant is represented as bearing our sins. Every great truth of the Gospel is anticipated in this prophecy. Date: 759–710 B.C.

Isaiah is called the *Evangelical Prophet.* The historical portion contains prophetic hints of Messiah's Glory; Birth of a virgin; manifold character. Cf. vi.; vii. 14; ix. 6, 7; xi. 1, 10; xxviii. 16; xxxii. 2. But at Chapter xl. there is an abrupt transition from the historical to the prophetical and Messianic portion. Then follows the fullest portrayal of Messiah's Person and Mission, humiliation and exaltation, to be found in the entire Old Testament. The *first five verses* of Chapter xl. are the germ of the whole twenty-seven chapters. To a sinning, suffering people, God's first message is *Comfort;* He has pardoned their sins. But pardon is not all. A Herald (John Baptist) is coming to prepare the Way of the Lord; and then shall follow a *new Revelation* of His glory, and *all Flesh* shall see it together. Here we have Reconciliation and Incarnation, Complete Revelation, and Universal Evangelization. Christ's death is so clearly foretold in Chapter liii., that Bolingbroke could evade its force only by claiming that Jesus brought on His own crucifixion by a series of preconcerted measures, merely to give His disciples the triumph of an appeal to prophecy!!

These twenty-seven chapters constitute *one grand Messianic Poem*, subdivided into three books; the first and the second end with the solemn refrain, " There is no peace, saith the Lord, unto the wicked "; and the third expresses the same thought more fully: " Their worm shall not die, neither shall their fire be quenched, and they shall be an abhorring unto all flesh." Each book consists of three sections of three chapters each, nearly corresponding with the divisions in our English Bibles:

Chap.	Chap.	Chap.
⎧ xl. ⎨ xli. ⎩ xlii.—xliii. 13.	⎧ xlix. ⎨ l. ⎩ li.	⎧ lviii. ⎨ lix. ⎩ lx.
⎧ xliii. 14—xliv. 5. ⎨ xliv. 6–23. ⎩ xliv. 24—xlv. 25.	⎧ lii. 1–12. ⎨ LIII. ⎩ liv.	⎧ lxi. ⎨ lxii. ⎩ lxiii. 1–6.
⎧ xlvi. ⎨ xlvii. ⎩ xlviii.	⎧ lv. ⎨ lvi. 1–8. ⎩ lvi. 9—lvii. 21.	⎧ lxiii. 7—lxiv. 12. ⎨ lxv. ⎩ lxvi.

The *fifty-third chapter is thus the middle chapter of the middle book of this great prophetic poem, the heart of the prophetic writings of the Old Testament.* And the *central verse of this central chapter enshrines the central truth of the Gospel:*

> "*He was wounded for our transgressions;
> He was bruised for our iniquities;
> The chastisement of our peace was upon Him;
> And with His stripes we are healed.*"

DIVISIONS: I.: i.—xxxix. Chronological and Historical. See i. 1.

II.: xl.—lxvi. The Song of Messiah.

JEREMIAH.

Key-word: WARNING.   ***Key-verse:*** VII. 28
XLVI. 1.

THIS Book of *bold rebuke* toward Judah and *prediction* against Gentile nations, is the trumpet-blast of a reformer in the ears of a perverse people, to whom twenty chapters of argument and appeal are vainly addressed. Here Messiah appears as The Branch, The King on David's Throne, The Lord our Righteousness; typically in Jeremiah himself, coming with a rejected message of repentance and salvation.

Judah needed the voice of warning. Declension followed Josiah's death; virtual paganism, with licentiousness and corruption, tainted even priests and prophets. *Superstitious rites* crept in: the worship of the Queen of Heaven, with Ishtar (Easter) cakes (vii. 17, 18; xliv. 18-26), and human sacrifices to Moloch.

Jeremiah, called in youth, held the prophetic sceptre for over forty years, B.C. 628 – 586. Nearly a hundred years lie between him and Isaiah. His warning rebukes, though tempered with tender entreaty, availed nothing. Jehoiakim burned his Roll and sought his life; and Hezekiah was vainly warned of the coming Captivity. The grandeur of his character appears in his fearlessness and faithfulness and passion for souls. He faced misrepresentation, persecution, the dungeon, and death, rather than keep back one word of the truth. Notwithstanding his heroism and gentleness, his bold rebukes made him hated. He was in a dungeon when Nebuchadnezzar took Jerusalem, went to Egypt with the remnant, and, according to tradition, was there stoned by his own countrymen.

DIVISIONS: I.: i.—xxxviii. Prophecies, etc., as to Judah, down to the Chaldean Invasion.

II.: xxxix.—xliv. Prophecy and History after Jerusalem's Fall.

III.: xlvi.—li. Prophecies against Egypt, Philistia, Moab, Ammon, Edom, Damascus, Kedar and Hazor, Elam and Babylon. Chapter xlv. is a fragment apparently out of place; lii. is an appendix

LAMENTATIONS.

Key-word: DESTRUCTION.   *Key-verse:* II. 11.

THIS is the minor strain of prophecy, a funeral dirge. The weeping prophet, whose life was one long martyrdom, fully identified with the sorrow of his people and the desolation of the Holy City, utters the wail of a broken heart. He sees the Chaldean army as the scourge of God chastising His wayward people: but even His judgments call them to return. Cf. Jesus weeping over Jerusalem. Luke xix. 41-42.

Note the *artistic arrangement* of this poem. It is an acrostic of singularly symmetrical structure. There are *five elegiac cantos.* In the first three Laments, each stanza is a triplet; in the fourth, each is a couplet. Moreover, in the third or middle, the climax of the poem, the three members of each stanza begin with the same letter; and the Revised Version properly arranges the sixty-six verses in groups of three each. In the fifth canto, the acrostic feature disappears, but there are twenty-two stanzas, corresponding in number to the letters of the Hebrew alphabet.

In the first Lament, Zion appears, a weeping widow in garments of mourning; in the three following, the poet-prophet, pathetically painting pictures of the ruin of the sacred capital. In the fifth, the People chanting mournfully, confess their sin, bewail their woe, and appeal to the Pity of God.

The "Grotto of Jeremiah," where tradition places him, as looking down upon the city and weeping over it, is shown on the hillside west of Jerusalem.

Jeremiah's vision of Jerusalem wasted and Babylon exulting, should be compared with John's vision of Babylon destroyed and the New Jerusalem revealed in triumph and heavenly beauty. Rev. xviii. Better to be one with Jerusalem in afflictions that issue in glory, than one with Babylon in the pride that ends in shame.

DIVISIONS: Five elegies, each a chapter. The first, second, and fourth, each subdivided into two equal parts, and the third into three. (1–18, 19–42, 43–66.) The subdivisions are easily detected by change of speaker and personal pronoun.

EZEKIEL.

Key-word: VISIONS. *Key-verse:* I. 1.

EZEKIEL, the Prophet of the Iron Harp, remarkable for energy of utterance, was a priest by line of descent. He is a pure SEER, who has visions of God. His pen is more conspicuous than his tongue, and his style is vivid and fervid. He sees the *Glory of the Lord,* records its departure from the city and Temple because of idolatry and iniquity, and, after national judgments, its Return in the latter day, and the national Resurrection of Israel.

The opening vision grandly represents the glory of the Lord, as seen in His works and word; in Creation, Providence, Scripture, Grace. The Ring resting on earth, its rim, full of eyes, reaching to heaven; the wheel within a wheel; the fourfold faces of the lion, calf, man, eagle,— may express the grandeur, sublimity, wisdom and power, complication and mystery of all His operations.

Isaiah and Jeremiah prophesied in Jerusalem. Ezekiel by the river Chebar, among the captives.

Jeremiah sketches the moral condition of God's people from the thirteenth year of Josiah's reign; Ezekiel, between the captivities of Jehoiachin and Zedekiah, the last two kings of Judah. He unfolds the *morale of the Captivity:* Law and Penalty; God's Judgment on idolatry and proud self-confidence; His instrument the Chaldeans.

Ezekiel should be compared with the other three major prophets, but particularly Daniel and with John in the Apocalypse over eighty points of contact will be found. The fourfold Living Creatures (Ζωα), seen in Ezekiel's vision, on earth, appear in John's, in heaven. Ezekiel sees the Church in judgment with Temple ritual; John, in Revelation, sees the Church in purity and victory with no Temple.

DIVISIONS: I: i.—xxiv. Introductory Vision, Commission as Prophet, Prediction of Jerusalem's Fall.

II.: xxv.—xxxii. Judgment of Ammon, Tyre, Egypt, Edom, Moab, Philistia.

III.: xxxiii.—xxxix. Warnings and Promises to Israel and Judah.

IV.: xl.—xlviii. Ideal Temple and City.

DANIEL.

Key-word: REVEALED SECRET. *Key-verse:* II. 22.

THIS Book is not properly a history of Jews, Babylonians, or Daniel, being continuous neither in matter nor in time of composition. Prophecy and history are intermingled; incidents, from a period of about seventy years, are chosen to illustrate the power of a fixed will, separation unto God, and the prayer of faith; God's interposition in miracle, inspiration in prophecy, Providence over kings and nations, and the Ministry of Angels.

The book is in *two equal parts:* the first is a *Narration;* the second, a *Revelation.* The Period is that of the Babylonish Captivity; Nebuchadnezzar at the summit of power, able but arrogant and despotic. In this very centre of Pagan World-power, Jehovah visits His exiles by miracle and prophecy, to show His Power and comfort them by glimpses of the Future.

The *Narrative* portion presents *conflict between the True God and False Gods,* in six forms:

1. Wisdom, or intellectual capacity; four Hebrew captives in competition with Chaldean sages.

2. Power to reveal Divine Secrets; Daniel's Prayer, not only discovering interpretations, but even disclosing dreams.

3. The worship of Jehovah *versus* idols; the three Holy Children delivered even from the ordeal of Fire.

4. Human *versus* Divine Sovereignty. Nebuchadnezzar's "I" succumbs to the great "I Am."

5. Sacrilege *versus* Retribution. Belshazzar's profane feast and the Awful Handwriting on the Wall.

6. Lower *versus* Higher Law. The Decree of Darius reversed, and Daniel taken unhurt out of the Den of Lions.

The *Apocalyptic* portion contains *two Dreams of World Empires,*—the Four Beasts, and the Ram and He-goat; Daniel's Prayer of Confession and the Answering Revelation; Angelic Ministries; prophecies as to Persia and Greece; and the Times before the End. The prophecies are thus in two classes: First, relating to Babylonian Monarchs, Nebuchadnezzar and Belshazzar; and secondly, Future Developments, embracing a general glance at World Empires which grew out of the Babylonian or Chaldean Monarchy then the almost single supreme Power, viz.

Medo-Persian, Macedonian or Grecian, and Roman. The four kingdoms of Chapter ii. and the four beasts of Chapter vii. are the same. Porphyry acknowledged the exact fulfilment of these prophecies, but said they must have been *written after the events!*

The Times of the Messiah are exactly given in Chapter ix. 24. It was seventy Heptades, or periods of seven, *i. e.*, 490 years, from the decree of Cyrus to the Messiah's Sacrifice and the sevenfold Finishing of His Atoning Work. (B.C. 455 to A.D. 33. As Christ was born from four to five years before the Christian era, as commonly reckoned, only 69 Heptades have been fulfilled. May not Daniel's 70th week be apocalyptic?)

Joseph in Egypt and John in Patmos strangely correspond to Daniel in Babylon. This book is full of mottoes for the young: "He would not defile himself," "An excellent spirit was in him," "He was faithful," "He believed in his God" "Stand in thy lot," etc.

DIVISIONS: I.: i.—vi. The **Conflict.**
II.: The Revelation, vii.—xii.

THE MINOR PROPHETS.

THESE twelve were classed by the Jews as one book (Acts vii. 42). By whom they were collected is not known, but Ezra, Nehemiah and Malachi may have aided in forming the canon. The period which they cover, within which the major prophets also fall, extends from about 870 to 440 B.C. The chronological order is about as follows: Joel, Jonah, Obadiah (?), Amos, Hosea, Micah, Nahum, Zephaniah, Habakkuk, (Obadiah?), Haggai, Zechariah, Malachi.

The *Division of the Kingdom* antedates Joel's day by more than a century. Hence, in these prophecies we meet the two kingdoms of Judah and Israel with their respective sins and judgments, calamities and captivities. Within this *most eventful era* in Hebrew history crowd an awful array of evils and disasters: calf-worship and idol-worship, forbidden marriages and foreign alliances, moral profligacy and religious apostasy, invasions from without and wars from within, captivities and restorations. The history must be placed side by side with the prophecy, for each interprets the other.

The prophecies contained in these twelve books present one complete view. The kingdom of David is seen as rent asunder, and its riven portions end in apparent ruin. But a believing Remnant always survives the wreck, and a Restoration will come when David's Son will rebuild the ruined nation and re-establish the throne. There is a constant Look Forward, past Macedonian conquests and Maccabean successes, the apostasy of the Jews and the destruction of Jerusalem; beyond even the dispersion of the elect nation, to the *Final Conversion* and *Ultimate Restoration of God's Chosen People.*

The Old Testament outline of Messiah and His Kingdom, which at earlier periods of prophecy was like a "drawing without color," now reaches completeness, and every prophetic book adds at least another touch or tint to the grand picture. David in the Psalms presents Messiah as Priest and King; Isaiah, as the obedient Servant, the suffering Saviour, the reigning Conqueror; Ezekiel, as the ideal Priest of an ideal Temple; Daniel, as the Prince, cut off without throne, people, or kingdom, but standing up at last on the ruins of the colossal World-Power. Zechariah presents him in all three offices, prophet, priest, king; and Malachi closes the canon with references to His first and second Advents.

Once let the reader of Prophecy get clear conceptions of this fact, that *Christ is its Personal Centre* and *Israel its National Centre*, and that around about these centres all else clusters and that in them all else converges, and, "whether he walks or runs, he will see all things clearly" for the vision is written in large letters as upon tablets by the wayside.

HOSEA.

Key-word. RETURN. *Key-verse:* XIV. 9.

THIS message is for the northern kingdom, Israel, of which Hosea was a native (?). The mortal throes of that kingdom were at hand; and Israel, rebuked as the faithless wife of a Divine Husband, is bidden to return from her backslidings unto Him. This unique *Ephraimite Book* scarce mentions Judah, and does not openly refer to Jerusalem. Hosea's period spans half a century.

This book is rhythmical; its language metaphorical and laconic. The nation was rotten with private vices and public crimes: lying and perjury, drunkenness and lust, robbery, murder, treason, and regicide. The worship of Jehovah was corrupted with idolatry and profaned by formality. Situated midway between Egypt and Assyria, two factions existed; one favoring alliance with Egypt, the other, with Assyria. The Kingdom of Israel had a brief period of prosperity followed by decadence and rapid ruin. There came violent changes on the throne; Assyria's first appearance in Palestine: finally Sargon took Samaria and Captivity ended the scene.

DIVISIONS: I.: i.—iii. The Marriage Covenant with Jehovah.

II.: iv.—xiv. The Stages of Decline: **the exhortation to Return.**

JOEL.

Key-word: JUDGMENT.   *Key-verse:* II. 13.

THIS Pioneer of the Prophets lived in Judah, probably in Jerusalem in the early days of Joash, B.C. 870–865. Locusts and Drought are used as symbols of swarms of invaders and dried-up national resources. He calls a FAST, to remove the present, and avert the threatened, Scourge; foretells prosperity, on condition of repentance, and the *Future Effusion of the Spirit*, the Latter Rain after drought.

Joel *speaks to Judah*, making no reference to Israel, or to idolatrous practices. The priests and people appear, as during Jehoida's priesthood, occupied with Temple-Service and Sacrifice. The Phœnicians, Philistines, Edomites, Egyptians have mention; but not the Babylonian, Assyrian, or Syrian invasions. Had he survived Joash, he would have noticed the last.

DIVISIONS: I.: i.—ii. 17. The Judgment, and Call to Repentance.

II.: ii. 18—iii. 21. The Promise for the Present and Future.

AMOS.

Key-word: PUNISHMENT.　　*Key-verse:* IV. 12.

LIKE his cotemporary, Hosea, Amos wrote for Israel, and denounces the same evils, foretelling overthrow by a foreign foe as the punishment for Israel's sins. The threats against the surrounding heathen, with which he begins, hold out no final hope; but Israel has Promise of New Deliverance and Prosperity under the House of David.

Amos, though a prophet of Israel, was a native of Judah, and a shepherd of Tekoa. Bethel was the scene of his ministry.

DIVISIONS: I.: i.—ii. Prophecies against Syrians, Philistines, Phœnicians, Edomites, Ammonites, Moabites, etc.

II.: iii.—vi. Against Israel.

III.: vii.—ix. Visions, Consolatory and Condemnatory, covering times previous to, and during Messiah's Reign.

OBADIAH.

Key-word: EDOM. *Key-verse:* 21.

BRIEFEST of the Prophecies, this covers the character, career, doom, and downfall of Edom or Idumæa. Esau's descendants were, to the last, the foes of Jacob's,—proud, bitter, resentful neighbors. Governed at first by Dukes, and afterward by Kings, they were in their golden age when the Israelites were at their Exodus. When Babylon assaulted the Holy City, Edom rejoiced to join the assault. Ps. cxxxvii. 7.

Of *Obadiah and his times*, we know nothing. His period is either before 800, or after 588 B.C. If he refers to the capture of Jerusalem, in the reign of Joram II., the earlier date is the correct one; if the period after Nebuchadnezzar's invasion be indicated, the later. This is less probable.

DIVISIONS: I.: 1—9. Judgment Announced.
II.: 10—16. Its Justification.
III.: 17—21. Promised Salvation to Zion.

JONAH.

Key-word: OVERTHROW.   *Key-verse:* III. 2.

THIS prophet of Israel was sent on a mission to the Gentiles. Nineveh, at the apex of pride and prosperity, was to be warned of coming and speedy downfall. Jonah rightly read mercy in his warning message, and his own vindictive waywardness drove him Westward instead of Eastward, until in the belly of a great fish he learned the lesson of obedience to God and pity for men.

The prophet was *out of sympathy with Foreign Missions.* His national prejudice construed God's election of Israel as a rejection of all others. His religious intolerance was mixed with no mercy for the heathen. His legal spirit inclined more to vengeance than to grace. His disloyal temper made him wilful and wayward, and compelled severe Divine correction.

To *refine away from this story* the *Supernatural* element destroys the product as an inspired book. It has been treated as a dream, fiction fable, parable, apologue, allegory; Jonah has been conceded to be a historical personage, treated in a symbolical character: representing in combination two kings of Judah, Manasseh and Josiah; the ship, the Jewish State, and the storm, a political crisis; the ship-master, the High Priest, Zadok; the great fish, Lybon on the Orontes where Manasseh was a prisoner. But such interpretations make havoc not only of the inspiration of the Word, but of the Divinity of our Lord, who treated this as a veritable narrative. Matt. xii. 39–41; xvi. 4.

The selfish unbelief and vindictiveness of man here contrast with the gracious patience and benevolence of God. The gourd illustrates the *Mediator*, needful to interpose between the head of the sinner and the insufferable Glory of the Holiness of God.

Divisions: I.: i. Jonah's Commission and Correction.

II.: ii. His Prayer and Deliverance.

III.: iii.—iv. His Commission renewed and discharged.

MICAH.

Key-word: CONTROVERSY.   *Key-verse:* VI. 2

MICAH speaks both to Samaria and Jerusalem, but mainly to Judah. As in all genuine prophecy, through present judgment future blessing appears. The Lord's *Controversy* with His people issues in infinite *Compassion.* Bethlehem, the Little, is preferred above Jerusalem, Mother of all, as the cradle of Messiah. He paints in unrivalled hues the character of Jehovah, who both *Passes over* transgressions and *overwhelms* them as in the sea. Cf. vii. 18–20. Exod. xii. 23; xiv. 27.

Micah was cotemporary with Isaiah and Hosea: his period, between 756 and 699 B.C. The sins he rebuked were the fruit of the unrestrained idolatry under Ahaz. The ruin of both kingdoms with their capitals will be followed by the Return of the Remnant, the restoration of the Jewish State and the Reign of Messiah. The word, "Hear," marks the divisions.

DIVISIONS: **I.: i.—ii.** Divine Visitation of Israel and Judah.

II.: iii.—v. The Desert of Sin and the Grace of the Last Days.

III.: vi.—vii. Jehovah's Controversy and Forgiveness.

NAHUM.

Key-word: FULL-END. *Key-verse:* I. 8, 9.

THIS is the Burden of Nineveh. Jonah's warning, perhaps a century before, had led to repentance; but judgment, *deferred*, is not *averted*. God will no longer spare: the threat of "overthrow" now changes to that of the *full-end*, annihilation. In images, never surpassed in the words or thought of man, the doom of the vast capital is portrayed.

As to the *person* and *period* of Nahum, he seems to have prophesied in Palestine somewhere between 712 and 685 B.C., in the latter part of Hezekiah's reign. He vividly and graphically describes Sennacherib's Assyrian army, whose last attempt to crush the Jews, in the 14th year of Hezekiah, met disastrous defeat. From fifty to a hundred years after this prediction, 625 B.C., the forces of Cyaxares and Nabopolasar overthrew Nineveh and Assyria.

HABAKKUK.

Key-word: FAITH.   *Key-verse:* II. 4.

THIS is the *Prophet of Faith.* He has a vision of the Coming Judgment of Judah by the Chaldean Invasion, but a more important vision of *Justification by Faith.* His name, "*Embrace,*" expresses the clinging trust that lays hold on God, and in his poem the central word and thought is FAITH, in its vital relation to righteousness and life's trials and triumphs. The Prayer with which this book closes touches the summit of the sublime.

"The JUST SHALL LIVE BY HIS FAITH." This is the significant vision which he was to make plain upon the tablets, such as were inscribed in large letters and set up in public places. This motto became the centre of Paul's doctrinal system. Rom. i. 7; Gal. iii. 11; Heb. x. 38. In Romans, JUST is the emphatic word; in Galatians, FAITH; in Hebrews, LIVE. When, to the Galatians, he refers to the "*large letters*" that he has written with his own "hand,"* he probably means this quotation from Habakkuk, the great sentence written in large characters upon the wayside tablets, and which afterward became the Creative sentence of the Great Reformation, written large by Luther, to be read by the whole race of man.

The probable date of the prophecy is 608–604 B.C., during the reign of Jehoiakim. The Chaldeans are about to invade Judea; God uses them as His Hammer to punish Judah, and then breaks the Hammer itself in pieces. Jer. l. 23.

Faith is the central figure, presented in all its aspects, the pledge and test of Righteousness, the fruit and proof of Life. It gives light in darkness, triumph in trial, peace in perplexity, stayed on the Word of God, the Rock of Ages. Isa. xxvi. 2, 3. In the entanglements of events, faith sees God working His own Will, and the final good of His People.

DIVISIONS: I.: i.—ii. The Prophet's Colloquy. He speaks, i. 2–4. God answers, 5–11. He speaks again, 12–17. He then takes a waiting attitude, ii. 1. God speaks again, 2–20.

II.: iii. The Prayer.

---

* Gal. vi. 11. Greek.

ZEPHANIAH.

Key-word: REMNANT. *Key-verse:* I 4; III. 13.

THIS "Compendium of all Prophecy," though addressed to Judah and Jerusalem, is a survey of Jehovah's universal government. The whole earth is the theatre where the Judge of all displays the grandeur of Law and the glory of Love. From every quarter, nations are chosen as examples of His just judgment, ii. 4-15. A *double " remnant"* is spoken of: a *remnant of Baal* that shall not escape; a *Remnant of Israel* that shall survive even judgment.

Zephaniah's *period* lies between 642 and 610 B.C. He predicts the overthrow of Assyria with Nineveh, and must have prophesied before 625 B.C., in the earlier part of Josiah's reign, when idolatries were partly destroyed, but a remnant of Baal remained. His message is *mainly to the Jews:* a rebuke of idolatry and depravity, and a warning of the Day of Jehovah, which is fourteen times referred to, in chapter i.

The glory of the Latter Day is foreseen, when all nations shall unite in the worship of the One God.

DIVISIONS: I.: i.—ii. 3. The Day of Judgment.
II.: ii. 4—iii. 7. The Provocation.
III.: iii. 8–20. The Salvation.

HAGGAI.

Key-word: BUILD.   *Key-verse:* I. 8.

HAGGAI heads the list of Post-Exile minor Prophets. He sounds God's call to an apathetic people to *rebuild His ruined Temple.* He contrasts the shame of their neglect with the reward of their fidelity. He promises that Jehovah will take pleasure in the work: the glory of the Latter House shall be greater than of the Former, for the Desire of all Nations shall come and tread its Courts.

In Ezra this book finds a historic, and in Zechariah a prophetic, Commentary. Haggai was probably one of the captives, returning under Zerubbabel, 536 B.C., and prophesied in the reign of Darius Hystaspis. The work of building, stayed through Samaritan influence with Smerdis the usurper, might have been resumed when Darius took the throne (521 B.C.), had not the sluggishness of an unfaithful people delayed it. Under the appeals of Haggai and Zechariah, the work again began in the second year of Darius, 520 B.C.

Haggai found some leaders of the people to whom prophecy proved not a tonic and stimulant, but a sedative and narcotic. Applying the "seventy years" to the *Temple* as well as to the *Exile*, they said that as yet but sixty-eight years had passed since its destruction, 588 B.C., and that the "*Time had not come* .... for the Lord's House to be built." So they let the Temple lie waste, while they built ceiled houses for themselves!

DIVISIONS: I.: i. The Exhortation.
II.: ii. 1–9. The Encouragement.
III.: ii. 10–19. A Message to the Priests.
IV.: ii. 20–23. A Message to Zerubbabel.

ZECHARIAH.

Key-word: JEALOUS.   *Key-verse:* VIII. 2.

ZECHARIAH is the *Prophet of the Advent.* Eight visions in one night unveil God's Providence and Grace toward the Elect Nation: her foes shall be destroyed, her idols removed, her City and Temple restored, and her Messiah revealed. If God's promises are to be enjoyed, His precepts must be obeyed, the Moral Law outranking the Ceremonial. Then Fasts become Feasts. Jehovah is *Jealous* for His people: His jealousy demands their purity and destroys their foes.

Zechariah, who stood by Haggai in urging the rebuilding, was, if Tradition be true, laid beside him after death. A priest by birth, and probably born in Babylon, he returned with Zerubbabel.

The book is in three parts. The first six chapters record the visions; the next two, God's answer concerning the Fast; and the last six contain predictions that reach to the Consummation of the Kingdom. They cover the Expedition of Alexander the Great, the Fall of Jerusalem, Jewish Dispersion and Final Conversion, Messiah's Advent, and the Great Feast of Tabernacles. The Confederacy that resists the re-establishment of the Jews in their own Land shall be broken in pieces; worship shall be restored in ideal purity, and even the Gentiles shall join in it. Messiah is twice referred to as the *Branch*, or Royal Stem.

DIVISIONS: I.: i.—vi. Visions.
II.: vii.—viii. Concerning Fasts.
III.: ix.—xiv. The Prophetic **Prospect.**

MALACHI.

Key-word: ROBBERY. *Key-verse:* III. 8.

MALACHI means "*My Messenger.*" He was sent to denounce practices that dishonored God and His Worship, and to strengthen the hands of Nehemiah in reforming abuses. His message closes the Old Testament. But through Four Centuries of Silence he foresees another *Messenger* who is to prepare the way of the Lord; and the advent of the Lord himself, the greatest Messenger of all, the "Angel of the Covenant."

This prophecy is of later date than Haggai, but belongs to the times of Nehemiah, 440–410 B.C., to whom Malachi bore a relation such as Haggai and Zechariah bore to Zerubbabel. In form it is a dialogue: the prophet's rebukes are met by rejoinders, which only evoke more scathing reproofs.

Robbery of God is its sad key-note. Idolatry had disappeared, but formality and hypocrisy had taken its place. The people withheld God's dues altogether, or nominally paid their holy obligations with worthless offerings. There was also Robbery of the poor, and the prophet with a scourge not of small cords lashes both priests and people.

The hollow formalism and complaining scepticism, here seen, are the germs of the Pharisaism and Sadduceeism that reached ripeness in the days of our Lord.

Love and Wrath are but different sides of one divine character. And so in this book of warning we find the crown of Old Testament *Promises*, iii. 10. Yet the last word of the Old Testament is "Curse." The Law and Ritual, the Captivity and its discipline, priesthood and prophecy, could not lift the Curse: there must be a fuller Revelation of Grace.

Prophetic silence reaches from Malachi to John Baptist, putting beyond doubt that prophecy was complete centuries before the events foretold. But there is a remarkable link between the two testaments: the last figures on the inspired page of Malachi, and the first on the inspired page of Matthew, are the Angel of the Covenant and His Forerunner.

DIVISIONS: I.: 1-5. Introductory Expostulation of Jehovah.

II.: i. 6—ii. 9. Rebuke of Priests.

III.: ii. 10–16. Rebuke of Divorce and mixed marriages.

IV.: ii. 17—iii. 6. The Coming Messenger.

V.: iii. 7–12. Tithes and Offerings.

VI.: iii. 13—iv. 6. **The Coming Day of the Lord.**

THE NEW TESTAMENT

Is not one book, but a little library of twenty-seven, by at least seven different writers, and the period of its production spans about half a century. There is no sign of collusion, yet there is no collision.

There is not only harmony, but *progress of doctrine.** Truths, found in germ in the Gospels, are historically illustrated in the Acts, doctrinally unfolded and applied in the Epistles, and symbolically presented in the Apocalypse.

This architectural plan is a proof of Inspiration. Even the order of the books has followed a divine purpose: it is *not the order of production*, but of the development and application of truth. Behind the seeming chances of history was God's plan determining the order of blocks in the building. Thus the Gospels present Christ in the four aspects of His Person and Work; the Acts show the Holy Spirit, as Christ's promised Paraclete, acting in the Church; the

---

* Bernhard, " Progress of Doctrine."

Epistles apply Christ's teaching to the details of holy life and growth; and the Revelation, like a dome, covers and crowns the whole structure.

The Law of *Comparing Scripture* with Scripture especially applies to these two Testaments. To read the Old with most profit, we must begin with the New; without understanding the Godhead of Christ and of the Holy Spirit, there is no true insight into the Old Testament. "Novum Testamentum in vetere, latet; vetus, in novo, patet."*

The Argument from *Fulfilled Prophecy* is particularly important, as it bears both on the Inspiration of the Word and the Divinity of Christ. The Old Testament contains three hundred and thirty-three predictions which converge in His Person, and in Him alone. To compare these *prophecies* of the Old Testament with the *histories* of the New, is enough to convince any candid mind that the Bible is the Word of God, and Jesus the Son of God.

---

* **Augustine.**

THE FOUR GOSPELS.

This Fourfold Story of Christ's Life is proven genuine by its harmonious testimony and undesigned coincidences. Each presents the subject from a different point of view, and the combination gives us, like a series of concentric mirrors, not an outline picture or a mere image, but a divine Person reflected, projected before us, like an object with proportions and dimensions.

Matthew wrote for the Jew, and shows Jesus as the King of the Jews, the Royal Lawgiver the *Lion* of the tribe of Judah. Mark wrote for the Roman, and shows Him, as the Power of God, the Mighty Worker, the *Ox* for service and sacrifice. Luke wrote for the Greek, and shows Him as the Wisdom of God, the human Teacher and Friend, the *Man* Christ Jesus. John, writing to supplement and complement the other Gospels, shows Him as Son of God, as well as Son of Man, having and giving Eternal Life, the *Eagle* soaring to the Sun, undazzled by its splendor.

These Four Gospels are the counterpart of

the *Four Living Creatures* (Ζωα) of Ezekiel, Daniel and the Apocalypse. Marvellously joined, intertwined with coincidences, yet separated by differences, they face different ways, yet move in one direction, as one Spirit guides; wing with wing, wheel within wheel, full of eyes, the scope of their rings dreadful, and their speed like that of lightning.

These are not Gospels *of* Matthew, etc., but *One Gospel of Christ, according to* Matthew, Mark, Luke, and John. The first three present the person and work of Christ from the outward, earthly side; the last, from the inward and heavenly. In the beginning of each gospel we find emphasized, in Matthew, Christ's genealogy; in Mark, His Majesty; in Luke, His Humanity; in John, His Divinity. So, in the close of each: in Matthew, His Resurrection; in Mark, His Ascension; in Luke, His Parting Benediction and Promise of Enduement; and in **John, the added hint of His Second Coming.**

MATTHEW.

Key-word: KINGDOM. *Key-verse:* XXVII. 37.

THIS recognized *Hebrew* Gospel is the true beginning of the New Testament, linking it with the Old. The New Covenant springs from the Old: hence the generation of Christ is traced back to David and Abraham. Messianic History fulfils Messianic Prophecy; hence the frequent reference to prediction. The Prophet, Priest, King, in whom Old Testament prophecies, ceremonies, and types meet, must be Messiah.

Matthew wrote in Palestine, in Hebrew, or Syro-Chaldaic, to the lost sheep of the house of Israel. He puts at the front the genealogy of Christ; the unit in the Bible is the Family. The Jews attached great importance to carefully kept tables of lineage, and there was a definite ancestral line in which Christ should come. Yet, even in that sacred line, we find aliens, Gentiles, and sinners, for He came to save such, and condescended with such to be identified. Between Abraham and Christ were three times "fourteen generations," or *forty-two*, the number of stations in the wilderness. Starting from Abraham

God's pilgrim people found no resting-place till they found Jesus.

Matthew proves the *Messiahship of Christ*, and so His *Kingship*, as David's son and successor. Hence the prominence given to the "*Kingdom of Heaven*": its announcement by John the Forerunner, then by Christ; its Beatitudes; conditions of entrance into and of greatness in it; the *seven* parables of the kingdom, which unfolded its mysteries (xiii.), and the *three* which present phases of the second advent (xxv.). Hence also the Kingly character of Christ is traced from His birth, and the worship of the Magi, through His kingly triumph over the Tempter, His Royal discourse on the Laws of His Kingdom, His majestic miracles, to His TRANSFIGURATION, as *the central event*, because it unveiled the *Full Glory of the Messianic King*. From this point, little is done or recorded, to prove the dignity and divinity of His Person, and He now begins to show the doctrine of His Vicarious Passion and Resurrection. xvi. 21.

DIVISIONS: I.: i.—iv. 16. From Christ's Birth to His Public Ministry.

II.: iv. 17—xvi. 28. His Public Ministry to His Transfiguration.

III.: xvii. 1—xxviii. 20. His Transfiguration to His Last Command.

MARK.

Key-word: SERVICE.   *Key-verse:* X. 45.

MARK is traditionally connected with Peter, who to the Romans opened the door of Faith (Acts xii. 12). This is the Gospel of the *Works of Christ* (Acts x. 38). Written for the Roman, whose watchword was *Power*, it exhibits Omnipotence in the mighty miracle-worker, and then the Omnipotence of Love in the crowning miracle of His Passion and Resurrection. The symbol of this Gospel is the Sacrificial *Bullock;* first at the plough in Service, then on the altar in Sacrifice.

The dominant idea of this Gospel is *Divine Power ministering to men*, and at the same time *attesting Christ's claims* as the Son of God. Hence Mark makes *miracles* prominent rather than Parables or discourses. After a brief introduction, he begins at once to record Christ's mighty works (i. 23). At least twenty of His most astonishing miracles are given in detail and in ten instances he adds general statements without entering into particulars (i. 34). Nearly half the chapters in this book close with some comprehensive summing up of His ministry of Power (cf. i., ii., iv., vi., vii., x., xvi.). Note especially the close of the Book itself.

Here, again, *the Transfiguration* is central. While Matthew emphasizes it as the revelation of the majesty of the King and glory of the *kingdom*, Mark characteristically adds, "*with power.*" (Cf. Matt. xvi. 28; Mark ix. 1.) After that revelation of the Divine Power of Christ, miracles fall into the background, only three being recorded.

Mark gives *no genealogy* or even an account of Christ's *Birth*, for he does not dwell on His descent either from Abraham or Adam. He exhibits the Son of God as Servant of both God and man, the *Ideal Levite*, first ministering before the altar, and then laying Himself upon the altar, completing His service by self-sacrifice.

DIVISIONS: I.: i. 1–20. Introduction: The Forerunner, Baptism, Temptation, etc.

II.: i. 21—viii. 38. His Miraculous Ministry.

III.: ix. 1—xvi. 20. From Transfiguration to Ascension.

LUKE.

Key-word: SON OF MAN. *Key-verse:* XIX. 10.

THE divinely perfect *Humanity* of the Son of God is here portrayed, and His genealogy traced, beyond David and Abraham, to *Adam*. This Divine Man, the second Adam, is, to Man as Man, Neighbor and Friend, Kinsman and Brother. But He is also the Lord from Heaven, the Divine Healer and Helper, Prophet and Saviour. Luke was Paul's friend and companion, and wrote especially for the *Greeks*, himself probably a Gentile proselyte.

Here the *Human Birth and Genealogy* of Christ are conspicuous, and the parables and miracles recorded touch universal humanity. He is seen going about doing good. Nearly one hundred passages in this narrative are *peculiar to Luke*. As the "beloved *physician*," many incidents would especially attract his notice. But the most of these peculiar features of this Gospel are due to his ruling purpose. He aimed to represent Christ as the *Wisest of*

Teachers and yet the *Best of Men*. Hence he gives prominence to such parables, miracles, and events as display His *matchless teaching* and His *identification with humanity*.

For example, Luke gives us the incident of the anointing of His feet by the woman who was a sinner (vii. 37-50), the story of Zaccheus, the affectionate warning to Simon Peter with the assurance of His prayer for him (xxii. 31, 32), the Promise to the Dying Thief, and the Interview on the Way to Emmaus; also the parables of the Good Samaritan, the Great Supper, the Lost Sheep, Lost Piece of Silver, and Lost Son (xv.); the Pharisee and Publican, and the Importunate Widow—which illustrate His tenderness and sympathy toward the neglected and outcast, the suffering and sinful, the publican and even the criminal. The *central chapter* is the Fifteenth, where by a group of *three parables*, the *Joy over the Lost, found*, is marvellously presented. The last words are a *Blessing*.

DIVISIONS: I.: i.—iv. 13. Introduction to Christ's Public Ministry.

II.: iv. 14—xxi. To the Last Passover.

III.: xxii.—xxiv. To His Ascension Blessing.

JOHN.

Key-word: LIFE. *Key-verse:* XX. 31.

This supplements the rest, settling all doubt as to the proper Divinity and Deity of Jesus as Son, not only of Abraham and Adam, but of *God.* John lived till the first heresies took shape. As Moses met all heresies about *Creation,* and led men back to its source in God, John met all heresies about the *Messiah,* Miracle Worker, Perfect Man, by declaring that in the Beginning the Word was, was with God, was God. Cf. Gen. i. 1, and John i. 1. The symbol of this Gospel is the *Eagle.*

"The Word" (λογος) is a fine title to be applied to the Lord Jesus, as the perfect expression of the perfect mind of God, the visible revealing the invisible. The Divine Nature, Eternally existent as spirit, exhibited in Creation, is fully *Manifested in the Flesh,* in Christ. The object of John is not polemic, but he indirectly antagonizes heresies, then developing, especially *gnosticism;* and, writing last, supplements the other Gospel narratives.

This Gospel touches the *Heart of Christ*. If Matthew corresponds to the Court of Israel, Mark to the Court of the Priests, and Luke to the Court of the Gentiles, John leads us past the veil into the Holy of Holies. Here is the inmost Temple, filled with the glory of God. The great theme is *Divine Manifestation* in Christ, as with Paul it is *Divine Reconciliation* through Christ.

Deep insight into the truth and person of our Lord; precious records of His discourses; the chosen metaphors of Christ, "I am the Bread, the Light—the Door,—the Good Shepherd— the Way, Truth, Life—Vine," etc., the Intercessory Prayer,—these are some of the peculiar attractions of the Fourth Gospel.

Life through Believing is declared to be the practical purpose of this book, and from the first mention of Life (i. 4) to the last (xx. 31) there will be found a gradual development of this great theme, every new reference to it adding some new thought.

DIVISIONS: I.: i. 1–18. Introduction. Prologue.

II.: i. 19—xii. Successive Manifestations to Jews, Samaritans, and Galileans.

III.: xiii.—xix Christ's Passion and Death.

IV.: xx.—xxi. Resurrection and Epilogue.

ACTS.

Key-word: WITNESS.   *Key-verse:* I. 8.

THIS book is the Gospels applied, the Acts of the Holy Ghost. Luke, in the Gospel, told what Jesus "*began*," and here what He *continued*, " both to do and teach " by the Holy Ghost, through disciples building up the Kingdom of God. The Door of Faith is opened successively to Hebrew, Roman, and Greek, as in the order of the Gospels. Pentecost links Old Testament Prophecy to New Testament History This is the Book of *Witness*, first of Man, secondly of God.

This is the *sequel to the Gospels*, the *basis of the Epistles;*—The Acts, not of the Apostles, but of the Holy Ghost and of the Risen Redeemer through the Promised Paraclete. The Holy Ghost applies the Truth and the Blood to penitent believers; then anoints them for service and sends them forth as WITNESSES to preach the kingdom, to make disciples and to organize them into churches. The author is Luke: the date about 63 A.D. (?), the time covered, about thirty-four years.

The Introduction refers to the **Forty Days of Communion** between the risen Lord and His disciples, which had a fourfold object and result. 1. To put His Resurrection beyond doubt; 2. To give instruction as to the kingdom of God; 3. To prepare them for His invisible conduct of the Church; 4. To inspire true missionary zeal.

Then follow the outlines of Church History. 1. The witnessing Church in *Jerusalem*, i. 13—vii.: Ten days of Prayer, PENTECOST and Preparation for Service, Persecution by Pharisees and Sadducees scattering disciples abroad; voluntary community of goods; Division of Labor and ordination of Deacons; the first martyrdom. 2. The witnessing Church in Judea and Samaria, viii.—ix. A Pentecost in Samaria under Philip the Evangelist. Simony — the Eunuch—SAUL of Tarsus. 3. The witnessing Church at the Ends of the Earth. A Gentile Pentecost at Cesarea; at ANTIOCH, the centre of the Gentile Church, and starting-point of Foreign Missions. Paul's three missionary journeys. The Book closes with Paul at *Rome*, the third great centre of Christianity. Paul is more conspicuous in the latter part of this book than Peter, because Peter went to the Dispersion, or Scattered Tribes of Israel. Gal. ii. 9.

THE EPISTLES

Form the "*Church-section*" of the New Testament. The Church, now founded both among Jews and Gentiles, needs the *Germs of Doctrine*, found in the Gospels, *amplified and applied*, for fuller instruction of believers, solution of practical problems and exposure of errors. This is done in the twenty-one Epistles.

There are *five writers*, each having his own sphere of truth. *Paul's* great theme is FAITH, and its relations to justification, sanctification, service, joy, and glory. *James* treats of WORKS, their relation to Faith as its justification before man. He is the counterpart and complement of Paul. *Peter* deals with HOPE, as the inspiration of God's pilgrim people in the temptations and trials of the wilderness. *John's* theme is LOVE, and its relation to the light and life of God as manifested in the believer. In his Gospel, he exhibits eternal life in Christ: in his Epistles, eternal life as seen in the believer. *Jude* sounds the trumpet of warning against APOSTASY; which implies the wreck of *faith*, the delusion of false *hope*, *love* grown cold, and the utter decay of good *works*

ROMANS.

Key-word: RIGHTEOUSNESS. *Key-verse:*
I. 17.

PAUL was peculiarly fitted for a great work among the Gentile nations, being by birth a Hebrew, by citizenship a Roman, by culture a Greek. He was divinely chosen to lay the foundations on which rests the whole scheme of Salvation. Righteousness or Justification is his theme. God's LAW is the only standard; God's Righteousness the only righteousness: by sin we have incurred condemnation; by faith we receive justification. All have sinned and come short; but the Righteousness of God by faith in Christ, becomes the righteousness of the believer.

Fourteen epistles are ascribed to Paul. Those to the Thessalonians belong first chronologically: this to the Romans, first logically and morally. It treats, like all his epistles, of *Faith*, but here faith *versus* law, *in relation to Justification*. It resembles that to the "Galatians." The Roman Church, mainly Jewish, trained in the Levitical code,—being prone to rely on conformity to Ritual and obedience to the Moral Law, and being in the Gentile Capital and Court of the World-Kingdom,—the argument must be framed to meet all false reliance on good works; and hence Paul begins by proving all under sin, and from the universality of Ruin, proceeds to the one way of Redemption for all.

Rome was one of the strategic points. "All roads led to Rome." This Epistle is fullest, most exhaustive and most fundamental. It is the open door to the treasuries of redemption. It was written about 58 A.D., at *Corinth*, where *wisdom* was the pride of the Greeks, to Rome where *law* was the boast; hence the fitness of addressing to Roman Christians a great argument on Man's position under the Law and Government of God. The whole tone of the Epistle is forensic, legal.

The emphatic words of the first part are from one root, δικη—δίκαιος, δικαιοω, δικαιωμα, δικαιωσις, δικαιοσυνη, δικαιοκρισια.

Divisions, mainly three: I.: i.—viii. Argument. Salvation by Faith in Christ alone. The whole world, Gentiles and Jews, condemned and guilty before God. Justification provided in Christ whose obedience and suffering avail the sinner who by faith is identified with Him.

II.: ix.—xi. Mutual Relations of Jew and Gentile and the two dispensations.

III.: xiii.—xvi. Practical duties, etc.

I. CORINTHIANS.

Key-word: WISDOM.   *Key-verse:* II. 7, 8.

CORINTH was the rival of Athens. The Greeks were proud of their language and literature, learning and logic ("speech" and "wisdom"). Paul prepares these Epistles to meet the Greek mind. He begins by renouncing wisdom, as to the Romans he renounced power. He magnifies the "things of God," "words of God," "demonstration of the Spirit," etc., and would not use wisdom of words lest the Cross be made of none effect.

This Epistle is throughout a rebuke to the princes of this world, confident in their worldly wisdom, but fools in God's sight. The world by wisdom knew not God. i. 21. The natural man does not, cannot, receive the things of the Spirit; the highest truths are veiled to him. Worldly wisdom cannot see in Christ crucified the Power and Wisdom of God. Justification by faith alone without reference to human merit, the sin of unbelief, Holy living by the power of Grace, Liberty in absolute submission to God, Prayer as an influence with God, Providence even in chastening—these are mysteries even to the sage. But all are revealed to believers by the Spirit. ii. 10.

The deepest of all these mysteries is the *mystical union between Christ and the Church*, and this is the key to the main divisions. *Factions in the Church* dishonor it. *Impurity* is destructive of it. *Marriage* illustrates it and is hallowed by it. *Identification with idols* profanes it. The *Lord's Supper* expresses and emblemizes it. *Disorderly Assemblies* disgrace it. The *Resurrection* consummates and crowns it. By virtue of this mystical union, the body of the believer becomes the Temple of God. Sin has defiled us. Deliverance comes only through the interpenetration of the believer's life with the divine life, in this union.

DIVISIONS: I.: i. 1–9. Introduction.
II.: i. 10—iv. 21. Church Factions.
III.: v. 1—vi. 20. Church Discipline.
IV.: vii. 1–40. Marriage and Celibacy.
V.: viii. 1—xi. 1. Meat offered to Idols.
VI.: xi. 2–34. Abuses in Church Assemblies.
VII.: xii. 1—xiv. 40. The Gifts of the Spirit.
VIII.: xv. Resurrection.
IX.: xvi. Sundry minor matters.

II. CORINTHIANS.

Key-word: COMFORT. *Key-verse:* VII. 6, 7.

HERE abound the *Contrasts of Sorrow and Joy,* of humiliation and exaltation. Paul had been sick nigh unto death and been healed; assailed as to his Apostleship and favored with the signs of an Apostle and even a rapture to the Third Heaven; judged of man, vindicated of God; harassed by the thorn in the flesh, sustained by all-sufficient grace. The key-note of the closing message, as of the opening salutation, is "*Comfort.*" Love, grieved by their sins, was comforted by their repentance. Cf. i. 3, 4; ii. 4; vii. 6, 7.

Paul's second visit to Corinth cost him much grief and humiliation. He found and rebuked sectarian schisms; he found and indignantly denounced Judaizing teachers; but he found also what most of all *grieved* him: *Heathen Immorality.* This was the cause of the pain, and the rumor of it was, perhaps, the occasion of the visit. This shocking immorality was upheld by an antinomian theory as to sensuality. He hesitated how to treat the evil: whether with mild or severe measures. iv. 21. The visit failed to attain its object, and the heathen vice rather increased.

Judaism had developed into a more organic form, and taken an attitude of more open, malignant hostility toward Paul. Impostors seem to have appeared, bearing letters of commendation from the mother church at Jerusalem (iii. 1–6, xi.), and to have derided both the Corinthian converts for their dissoluteness, and the Apostle for his incompetency to deal with it. They denied his apostleship, and met his gospel of a *Christ after the Spirit, the Son of God* with another gospel of a *Christ after the flesh, the Son of David;* they obscured faith, and insisted on obedience to the Mosaic law. Both Epistles seem written in the same year, 67 A.D.

The most complete argument on *giving* may be found in chapters viii.—ix.

GALATIANS.

Key-word: FAITH. *Key-verse:* III. 11.

THIS Epistle was written to set forth *Grace* in contrast to *Law*, and *Faith* in contrast to *Works*. Here for a second time we find the great centre of Paul's doctrinal system: "*The Just shall live by* FAITH," with *Faith* now the emphatic word. The Epistle is full of contrasts: the Flesh and its works, the Spirit and His fruits; Circumcision and New Creation; the World and the Cross.

Paul first preached in Galatia; on his second visit three years later, he found a party had taught a mischievous legalism, and this false doctrine he vigorously attacks. After a vindication of his Apostolate, as having the seal of God and the recognition of those who were Pillars in the Church, he enters at once upon his argument. ii. 15. From first to last *Faith* is the *condition of Justification*, and even faith is of grace. He warns against a relapse into the bondage of legalism, as a reversal of the Gospel.

False teachers had perverted the Old Testament to uphold legalism. He shows its true teaching. To Abraham grace was revealed and faith was counted for righteousness. The law cannot justify; it condemns; it is preparatory to Grace,—our pedagogue to lead to Christ. The Law dealt in outward ordinances, such as circumcision and Levitical ceremonies; and had an outward Temple with its ritual, fasts, feasts, and festivals. In Christ we pass from children to sons, from minority to majority, from bondage to liberty in conscious sonship and heirship.

But liberty is not license. *Faith* has its fruit in *works* of Love. The flesh and the spirit are each manifested by the life. The Cross which is the hope of Justification is the pledge of sanctification. The law of salvation is the same, both from the penalty and from the power of sin. Those who find antagonism between the Epistles of *Paul* and *James*, should study this, "to the Galatians."

DIVISIONS: threefold, each of two chapters
I. Paul's Apostolate; Salvation by Grace.
II. The Bondage of Law.
III. The Liberty of Sons.

EPHESIANS.

Key-words: IN CHRIST, ONE. *Key-verse:* I. 3.

IN this Epic of the New Testament is first clearly brought out *Identification with Christ.* The Believer is *in* and *with* Christ. Comp. 1 Cor. iii. 21. The Church, as the *Building* of which He is corner-stone, the *Body* of which He is Head, the *Bride* of whom He is Bridegroom, is One with Him and inseparable from Him. The Saints are exhorted to such a life as consists with this high calling, and the "Mystery" is specially magnified, of the *Incorporation of the Gentiles* into this sacred Unity.

Note the *progress of doctrine*, in the development of this idea of the believer's oneness with Christ. Matt. i. 23. "Emmanuel: God with us." Matt. x. 40; xxv. 35. Acts ix. 4. Then note the progress of *Figurative expression.* John x. 1–29. *Sheep* and *Shepherd;* xv. 1–8. *Vine* and *Branches;* now in Ephesians, ii. 20–22. *Building* or Temple; iv. 12–16. *Body* and *Members;* v. 32. Bride and Bridegroom, most sacred union known to man. Again, this union is asserted in most positive terms, unveiled by symbol or figure. Jno. x. 14, 15 (Revision); xvi. 26, 27; xvii. 21, 22, 23, 26. In this Epistle the practical phases of this truth are set forth. Christ's life is representative and typical: *In Him* the believer has his true probation, justification, sanctification; *In Him* is born from above, circumcised, baptized, anointed; is dead, buried, risen, and prospectively glorified. Cf. 1 Jno. iv. 17.

Paul resided at Ephesus three years, and fully preached the Gospel there. Acts xix. 8, 10; xx. 31; Rev. ii. 1–7. There were Satan's camp and court, Diana's Temple, Demetrius and the Silver Shrines, Magical Books, etc.

The theme of the Epistle is electing grace: Christ in the flesh dying, reconciling God and man, also man and man; the mystery, glory, blessedness of the Church as His *Body* and *Bride*. IN HIM WE ARE AND HAVE ALL. The Epistle reaches the summit of sublimity of revelations; it is Paul's *third heaven* epistle. In it he soars from the depths of ruin to the heights of redemption, see key-verse: $\varepsilon v\ \tau o\iota s\ \varepsilon \pi o v \rho a v o \iota s\ \varepsilon v\ X \rho \iota \sigma \tau \omega$.

DIVISIONS: I.: i.—iv. 16. Origin, Institution, Purpose, of Christ's Universal Church.

II.: iv. 17—vi. 10. Ethical Duties: Truth, Purity, Love, Marriage, Service.

III.: vi. 10–24. Concluding Exhortation. Panoply of God, etc.

PHILIPPIANS.

Key-word: GAIN. *Key-verse:* III. 7, 14; IV. 4

This Epistle is the disciple's *Balance-sheet.* Paul puts on one side all that was *gain* to him, and which he counted *loss* for Christ. Then he puts on the other side all that he won by the surrender, and will yet know and attain, and he finds himself infinitely richer. He forgets all he has forsaken, and presses on for the *prize.* "To live is Christ; to die is *gain.*" Cf. i. 21; iii. 7, 14.

This is simply a letter to the church at Philippi, founded by Paul and linked with Lydia and the Jailer. No doctrinal or practical error is rebuked. But the Apostle shows the *Renunciations* and *Compensations* of a disciple, and the infinite excess in his favor. His key-note is "*Rejoice in the Lord alway, and again I say, Rejoice!*" Some twenty times in the Epistle he uses the words, "joy," "rejoice," "peace," "content," etc. The Cross is forgotten in the Crown which is anticipated even in his earthly experience.

The supreme idea of the Epistle is GAIN. His zealous love for Philippian Christians brings gain to him, for it makes him magnanimously forget his bonds. The supremacy of Christ in his heart brings gain, for it helps him to rejoice whenever and by whomsoever Christ is preached, and turns all self-denial into abounding joy; it transforms a life of privation into privilege, and death into gain. He rejoices in Heavenly Citizenship (iii. 20, Greek), and in having the Mind of Christ. He shows how there is the *Gain* also of constant *Christian Progress;* and the Goal of all, the highest gain, is the *Out-Resurrection* from among the dead ($\varepsilon\xi\alpha\nu\alpha\sigma\tau\alpha\sigma\iota\varsigma$.)

The Epistle was written from Rome to Philippi, a colony (Acts xvi. 12), about A.D. 63.

DIVISIONS: I.: i. 1--26. Paul's Love and Joy.

II.: i. 27—ii. 30. The Heavenly Citizen and his Privileges.

III.: iii. Christian Progress.

IV.: iv. Six Practical Exhortations.

COLOSSIANS.

Key-word: IN CHRIST, COMPLETE. *Key-verse:* II. 10.

This Epistle shows the SAINTS, IN CHRIST JESUS, COMPLETE, and their standing and privilege, rights and riches, *in Him.* First the *Deity of Christ* as the Image of God is set forth; then his *Dignity* as Head of the Body, and His *Identity* with the Church; then, the consequent Dignity of the Church, and Identity with Him and in Him with the Father. Pre-eminence is His, the true *Pleroma* or Plenitude of Being, and of this Pleroma all saints in Him partake.

Colosse was a town of Phrygia, near Laodicea; the church was neither founded nor visited by Paul. Epaphras, a Colossian, reported the condition of the church to Paul during his first imprisonment in Rome, and Paul wrote to Colosse A.D. 63.

This Epistle is the companion to that *to the Ephesians.* In both, the theme is *the Saints in*

Christ Jesus: in Ephesians, they are seen to be *One in Him;* in Colossians, *complete in Him.* But in both Epistles the same lofty themes are treated: The Mystery of God, Headship of Christ, the Old and New Man, etc.

This Epistle is marked by its *Christology.* Its tone is polemic: combating a semi-Jewish Mysticism, a false Asceticism; a Gnosticism with a false Cosmogony, Adoration of Angels, and misleading Wisdom. There was an early controversy about the *Pleroma,* or Fulness of Being and source of all other Life. Here this Pleroma is claimed for Christ pre-eminently, and in Him for all saints, as members of the Body of which He is the Head. It implies *fulness of knowledge* ($\epsilon\pi\iota\gamma\nu\omega\sigma\iota\varsigma$, i. 9), of life, of spiritual state and standing, and resurrection glory, etc.

DIVISIONS: I.: i. 1–12. Opening Salutation and Prayer.

II.: i. 13—ii. 5. The Doctrine of the Epistle: *The Saints in Christ.*

III.: ii. 6—iv. 6. Practical Exhortations based on this Doctrinal Teaching.

IV.: iv. 7–18. Closing Salutations.

I. II. THESSALONIANS.

Key-word: WAITING. *Key-verse:* 1 Thess. I. 10
2 Thess. III. 5.

THESE two Epistles both treat of the *Second Coming* of our Lord, its antecedent and consequent events. They rebuke Thessalonian Materialism, which inscribed on tombs, "Death is an Eternal Sleep";* they correct mistakes as to the dead saints, and the Man of Sin. Two aspects of Christ's Second Advent are here plainly presented: in the first, He comes with the trump of God to raise the dead in Christ and catch up the living saints; in the second, He comes with His mighty angels taking vengeance on His foes.

Thessalonica was a historic city. In the first century the most populous in Macedonia; be

---

* Literally. "After Death no reviving,
After Grave no meeting."

fore the founding of Constantinople, virtual metropolis of Greece and Illyricum; it is even now the second city of European Turkey. It was one of the starting-points of the Gospel, and as such became more conspicuous than Antioch. The third century was its heroic age, and it was the mediæval Bulwark of the Faith.

Greece was at this time in two provinces, *Macedonia* and *Achaia;* of the former, *Thessalonica* was the capital; of the latter, *Corinth.* Thessalonica was an influential centre, having a fine harbor, and connected with Asia, eastward, and the Adriatic and Italy, westward. Paul first preached there on his tour into Greece in his second missionary journey, but was driven out, and went to Berea, etc.

Both Epistles are dogmatic—they present the true faith in opposition to doctrinal and practical error. In the first Epistle, he commends the Thessalonians for an example that was itself the highest evidence of Christianity, refers to his own apostolic authority and affection, affirms Christ's death, resurrection, and second advent; the Resurrection of the Dead in Christ, etc. In the second, he shows that the Parousia of the man of sin must precede the Epiphany of the Parousia of Christ, which is the signal for his complete overthrow. 2 Thess. ii. 8.

In no epistles is the *Lord's Coming* so conspicuous, as the object of the "Patience of

Hope." Saints are to be in the constant attitude of watching and waiting for an event always *imminent*—*i. e.* liable to occur at any time, certain at some time. Hence saints are "to wait for His Son from Heaven" (i. 10) as those "called to His kingdom and glory" (ii. 12), and who are to be the glory and joy of the apostle, at His Coming (ii. 19). They to be unblameable in holiness, at His coming with all His saints (iii. 13). They are not to sorrow, as others who have no hope, for the dead in Christ, who sleep in Jesus and are to come with Him, iv. 14, etc. The two Epistles contain twenty distinct references to the Second Coming, which is used as a comfort in bereavement, a motive to patience, an inspiration to hope, a security in temptation, a help to purity, a ground of rejoicing, a separating, sanctifying Power.

DIVISIONS: In the first Epistle, the first three chapters are personal and historical; the last two, didactic and hortatory.

In the second, the first chapter presents consolation under persecution; the second (1-12), the consummation of evil, and at verse 13, begin the closing exhortations.

I. II. TIMOTHY.

Key-word: DOCTRINE. *Key-verse:* 1 Tim. III. 9
2 Tim. I. 13.

THE Epistles to Timothy, like that to Titus, are called *pastoral* because addressed to individuals in charge of the flock. The object of these two Epistles is to leave a legacy of Apostolic warning and counsel for the direction and comfort of the Church. To Timothy Paul sustained peculiar relations, as to his son in the faith, and in these letters he makes very emphatic the need of *sound doctrine.*

The *special error* herein attacked is the *Gnostic Heresy;* and *six features* of this false doctrine are here prominent: 1. The claim to *superior knowledge,* insight, illumination (γνωσις, επιγνωσις). 2. A *spurious theory* of religion, with profitless and barren speculation. 3. A *practical lawlessness,* cauterizing the conscience as with a hot iron. 4. An *allegorical interpretation* of Scripture, explaining away the resur rection, etc. 5. An empty *form of godliness*, in which words took the place of works. 6. A *compromise* between God and Mammon, reducing godliness to a matter of trade or worldly gain. 7. Withal, a *pretence of superior sanctity*, that licensed even flagrant sins by profession of a pure motive.

The *moral guilt of heresy* is here emphasized, and the necessity of shunning vain speculation, that substitutes fables for facts, and strifes of words for holy works. Doctrine is uniformly asso ciated with spiritual health and vigorous activity. Cf. υγιαινουσα διδασκαλια, υγιαινοντες λογοι, υγιης λογος. 1 Tim. i. 10; vi. 3. 2 Tim. i. 13; iv. 3. Cf. Titus i. 9, 13; ii. 1, 2, 8.

These Epistles are associated with *Paul's imprisonment* at Rome. He dwelt two years in his own hired house, till the spring of A.D. 63. In July, 64, there was a seven-days' fire at Rome, that burned ten of the fourteen regiones of the capital. Nero, to divert suspicion from himself, charged it on Christians. Paul was in prison for two years, then liberated, and journeyed perhaps to Spain and Britain. In his second incarceration he was treated with greater severity, persecution being then begun. During this second imprisonment, Paul wrote this second Epistle, which was also his last; and suffered martyrdom some time previous to Nero's death, which was in June, 68 A.D.

Paul, like his Master, bore the burden of loneliness and consciousness of approaching martyrdom, but like his Master he forgot himself, and urged Timothy to the diligent use of the gift of God. He foresaw coming apostasy, and false teachers; but he encouraged him by *four* grand motives: 1. The verity and certainty of sound doctrine. 2. The mutual Testimony of Christ and the Scriptures. 3. The approval of the Master. 4. The coming Epiphany of Christ and the Day of Award.

TITUS.

Key-word: PROFITABLE.   *Key-verse:* III. 8, 9

THIS letter is *official* rather than personal. It is addressed to an uncircumcised Greek, of all the fellow-workers of Paul, least a Jew in character and sympathy. The fidelity and sagacity of Titus led Paul to trust him with special missions, and to leave him in Crete as his own representative, to complete the organization of Churches. Short and practical, this Epistle embodies two rich and comprehensive outlines of Salvation by Grace: ii. 11–14; iii. 4–8.

This Epistle is mainly occupied with Church *order, ordination,* and *organization.* Instructions are given as to primitive Episcopal superintendence. Presbyters and bishops are used as equivalent terms; and their qualifications are indicated, particularly a godly self-control and household rule, unblemished character, untarnished reputation, soundness of doctrine, and aptness in teaching.

Exhortations are addressed to various classes in the Church. Even slaves are taught that they may adorn (κοσμῶσιν) the doctrine of God our Saviour in all things. All disciples may be not only epistles, but illustrated and illuminated epistles of grace, and all this, even among the Cretians, who are described as *false, fierce, gluttonous*. i. 12. The Gospel that can transform them even into blameless bishops, and make even their slaves an ornament to the truth, must be profitable indeed.

The passage ii. 11–14 is one of the "loca classica" of Scripture. It covers past redemption, present duty, future glory. It is a table of contents to the entire New Testament: the Epiphany of Grace well describes the Gospels and Acts; the instructions in holy living, the Epistles; and the expectation of the coming of the Lord, the Apocalypse.

DIVISIONS: These mainly follow *the chapters*. The first is mainly occupied with the qualifications of a bishop or elder; the second, with the need of sound doctrine; and the third, with the need of good works.

PHILEMON.

Key-word: RECEIVE (Intercession). *Key-verse:* 17.

IF " Ephesians is the Lyric," Philemon is "the Idyl of the New Testament," combining beauty with brevity. Onesimus was a slave who had stolen, and then run away, from Philemon. Converted, baptized, cherished by Paul, he was by him sent back to his master, whom the Apostle besought to *receive him* no longer as a slave but a brother, and to put to Paul's account any wrong he had done him as master.

Philemon seems to have been affluent in circumstances, and hospitable toward saints. Onesimus means *profitable.* Paul plays on the name, acknowledging that he had been very unprofitable, but was now profitable to them both, as a renewed man, and had, by ministering to Paul in his bonds, endeared himself to him so as to become as his own vital organs. He therefore becomes intercessor for the slave and thief, and beseeches Philemon for his sake to receive him, counting him no longer either a bondservant or a transgressor; and the Epistle is especially rich in expressions of *Paul's identification* with this converted slave, who was to him, his *son*, his own bowels, his brother beloved, his second self.

No epistle is richer in *typical teaching*. We have here in profile an illustration of the *whole scheme of redemption*. "I BESEECH THEE RECEIVE HIM." Roman Law gave the slave no right of asylum, but conceded one right, that of appeal. He might flee to his master's friend, not for concealment but for intercession. The owner was absolute, but might be *besought* through a friend whom he counted as a *partner*, and the slave who fled thus to an intercessor did not incur the guilt and penalty of a fugitive. Again, the Roman Law provided for a slave's *manumission:* he might be adopted by his master as a son and so be freed. This short Epistle is full of references to these facts which conditioned Roman slaves.

The illustration becomes almost an analogy when applied to the sinner. He is God's property, but he has not only run away from his Master, but robbed Him. The Law affords him no right of asylum, but grace concedes him the right of appeal. He flees for refuge to Jesus, whom God counts a partner. *In Him* he is begotten anew as a son, and finds both *precator*, an intercessor, and *genitor*, a begetting father; *from Him* he returns to God, and is received not as a runaway slave and thief, but as a brother beloved, as Christ himself, and all the debt that he owes to God is put to Christ's account. Here is both intercession and manumission.

DIVISIONS: I.: Salutation and Prelude. 1-7.
II.: Request and its basis. 8-17.
III.: The Settlement and Signature. **18, 19.**
IV.: Epilogue.

HEBREWS.

Key-word: BETTER. *Key-verse:* XI. 40.

This Epistle to Hebrew disciples is attributed to Paul. They were in danger of *going back* to Judaism, and he seeks to prevent this by showing that in every respect the Christian faith and Church mark a great advance upon the Jewish. The Epistle adapts itself especially to a period of persecution, and exhorts and encourages these Jewish converts to *let go* everything else, but *hold fast* the faith and hope of the Gospel.

Remarkable unity characterizes this Epistle. Its one idea is to restrain Hebrew Christians from abandoning their new faith. Judaism, perfect as it seemed in its time and for its purpose, is superseded by a greater and better system. The argument branches into *three* divisions: *Christ is superior*—1. To angels employed at Sinai, as messengers. 2. To Moses, the greatest of human mediators, legislators, and leaders. 3. To Aaron, with the whole economy of priesthood, temple, and offerings. Christ was made *lower* than the angels, in order to *die;* but by resurrection exalted again *higher* than they who are but messengers to do His will, and minister to heirs of salvation while He sits on the very throne of God. Christ was far superior to Moses, who was but a servant, while He is the Son and Heir; and so, to Aaron and his fellow-priests who were sinners, were many, and served but for a time, and needed to make new offerings and sacrifices every year, since He is sinless, abides a priest only and continually, and once for all obtained eternal redemption. Christ ministers in a higher sanctuary, offers a better sacrifice.

The word *Better* occurs thirteen times in this Epistle: Christ, the better hope, the better substance, the better country, the better covenant and promises, sacrifices, resurrection, etc. The *idea* permeates the whole Epistle, and gives great force to the concluding exhortation to *hold fast* (x. 23), and to the awful warning as to the terrible results of apostasy, or *drawing back* (x. 32-39).

DIVISIONS: I.: i.—x. 18. The Grand *Argument.*

II.: x. 19—xiii. 25. Practical Exhortations and Admonitions.

JAMES.

Key-word: WORKS. *Key-verse:* II. 26.

THIS is the Epistle of *Holy Living*. Great stress is laid upon works, not apart from faith, but as both the proof and fruit of faith. It opposes Antinomianism. There is a morality-side to the Gospel. The disciple is under Law though justified by faith. Obedience is his watchword, the Obedience of Faith. Where grace inwardly dwells, there will be a Temple purified from all uncleanness.

The author was doubtless James, Bishop of the Church at Jerusalem, who seems to have been an ascetic if not a Nazarite. He was distinguished for practical piety; his knees were said to be callous from constant intercession for the sins of the people; and he has received the title, not only of ὁ δικαιος, the Just one, but Ωβλιας, Bulwark of the People.

This Epistle is addressed to the *Twelve Tribes of the Dispersion.* It has an air of patriarchal authority, as from the Father of the Church at

Jerusalem. It is in tone of thought, feeling, and language, thoroughly Hebrew.

More than any other Epistle it deals with the *external life.* The word of God is a *mirror* to show us what manner of man we are, and to influence character and conduct. The only true hearer of the word is the doer of the work. Life is a scene of temptation, demanding struggle and heroic endurance. Business plans are to be but the practical carrying out of God's will,—a vocation, not an avocation. We are to exhibit an unworldly type of character, avoiding not only intimate friendship, but contaminating contact, with the world. On the other hand, we are to cultivate Christian fellowship—discountenancing *caste,* restraining the *tongue.* Every true inward grace bears outward fruits: the wisdom from above, Faith, the Royal Law of Love; even Prayer is energetic—it works results. Pure religion ($\theta\rho\eta\sigma\varkappa\varepsilon\iota\alpha$, religious observance, worship, ritual) is to visit the fatherless and widows, etc.

Paul and James do not conflict. They stand not face to face, beating each other, but back to back, beating off common foes.

I II. PETER.

Key-word: "PRECIOUS." *Key-text:* 1 Pet. II. 7.*

THESE Epistles were addressed "to the Elect Pilgrims of the Dispersion," *i. e.* not to the Gentile churches, nor to the Hebrews who still clung to the Holy City and its Temple; but to those who had renounced Judaism for Christ and the earthly Canaan for the Paradise on high. Paul went to the Gentiles westward, Peter to the scattered tribes eastward. See Gal. ii. 9. These letters are meant to comfort these Hebrew converts under the approach or outburst of persecutions, help them to a godly life in this trial and test of faith among evil men, and exhibit the government of God toward them and over the world.

Peter is the Apostle of *Hope*, as Paul is of *Faith*, John, of *Love*, and James, of *Action*. The first Epistle was written from Babylon (v. 13).

Seven "precious" things are presented in these Epistles: viz.: The trial of *faith*, the

---
* Literally: "He is the Preciousness!"

blood, the *Living Stone*, *Christ* himself, the *faith*, the *promises*, the *meek and quiet spirit*. Compare 1 Pet. i. 7, 19; ii. 4, 6, 7; iii. 4; 2 Pet. i. 1, 4. The central passage of the seven is 1 Pet. ii. 7, the key of the whole Epistle. These Epistles closely resemble " Hebrews " and "Jude."

The line of thought is as follows: The position of the Christian believer is first contrasted with that of the Judaist. Israel's rejected Messiah is then shown to be the Headstone of the Corner, and the Elect of God to be the true heirs of hope. Then the disciple is viewed in his service and suffering as under God's providential and gracious care; Christ is set forth as an example; His vicarious death, our salvation. *God is judge*, and will begin with His own nominal " House."

Important thoughts: *Pilgrimage;* the disciple is at once a pilgrim, stranger and sojourner. Comp. Heb. xi. 13-16. *The Christian's place in this world*, as in Paul's Epistles; the Christian's place on high and in the world to come.

The second Epistle was written in expectation of shortly "putting off his tabernacle." Peter is said to have been crucified, and at his own request with head downwards. Peter sketches the *iniquity*, as Jude does the *apostasy*, of the "last days." Here the government of God over the *world* is more prominent, and His final *judgment of this world*.

I. JOHN.

Key-word: FELLOWSHIP.   *Key-verse:* V. 13.

THIS is a general epistle, not to any local church, drawing no line between Jew and Gentile; written about 90 A.D., John being the only surviving Apostle. Its tone is *paternal*, both in authority and affection; and *prophetic*, having an air of final decision and declaration. Its thoughts cluster about three grand centres: *Light, Love,* and *Life.* Its object is that believers may "know that they have eternal life, and so their joy may be full." i. 4; v. 13.

The book shows John's mental habit, contemplative rather than argumentative, confident of truth, taught by intuition, confirmed by experience. The "Apostle of Love" is still Boanerges, thundering against heresies that assail Christ's divine mediatorial character. Love is not laxity.

The Gospel of John shows **sinners how to**

get eternal life by believing: the Epistle shows believers how to know that they have eternal life. Sonship in Christ is unto heirship of life, and there are plain features by which the son and heir of God is to be known. The comprehensive test is FELLOWSHIP. (Κοινωνια or " having all things common," Acts iv. 32.) This fellowship is both with God and with the godly, i. 3; and is marked by three conditions:

1. God is *Light*. Light stands for truth, purity, knowledge, and joy. The believer has no fellowship with a lie, with what is evil and vile. He confesses sin, is cleansed by the blood, and kept by the advocacy of Christ.

2. God is *Love*. He loves holiness with pure complacence, and souls with pure benevolence. Love implies hate of all sin. The believer has fellowship in this love, and dwells in it. It is a law of his life. He loves God for what He is, and the godly for the godlike in them.

3. God is *Life*. Life, opposed to Death, is the very principle of antagonism to evil and assimilation to good. The law of the new life is obedience. Seeds of evil still exist in the child of God: but they should not *germinate*, and cannot *dominate*, for God's seed is in him. There is, therefore, a new *Affinity*, Regeneration; a new *Attitude*, Resistance to evil; a new *Advance*, toward perfection. The results of such fellowship are a twofold witness to sonship, *ex-*

ternal and *internal*, the witness of the Word and the witness of the Spirit.

DIVISIONS: I.: i. 1–4. Introductory. The Logos: His Eternity and Identity with the Father: His revelation in the flesh.

II.: i. 5—ii. 11. The Message concerning Light.

III : ii. 12—v. 3. The Message concerning Love.

IV.: v. 4–21. The Message concerning **Life**

II. JOHN.

Key-word: WALK (in Truth).   *Key-verse:* **6.**

LIKE Paul's to Philemon, this is a private personal letter, addressed to an unknown Christian woman and her pious family. It belongs to the *time,* and bears the *tone,* of the first Epistle. It sets a high value on the piety of a mother and her household; and warns against the abuse of hospitality by those who would undermine holy living and propagate error. It is a tribute to the Dignity of Womanhood, Wifehood, and Motherhood.

Here Home and Household are *honored* as spheres of service. Woman is tempted to envy the wider public sphere of man. But her hand is on the potter's wheel where vessels are shaped for the master.

Here Home and Household are *guarded.* John warns us against those who not only err in doctrine, but who sow the seeds of heresy and iniquity. Hospitality is not forbidden, nor courtesy; but proper guards are placed about a home where evil teachers might work **great harm.**

III. JOHN

Key-word: FELLOW-HELPER (to the Truth).
Key-verse: 8.

THIS letter is somewhat like the other but it is to a man, addressed by name, probably the Gaius who was Paul's convert and host. 1 Cor. i. 14. Rom. xvi. 23. As, in the second letter, hospitality was forbidden toward propagators of error, here it is especially encouraged toward promulgators of the truth. The elect lady was warned not to be partaker of their evil deeds; here Gaius is praised as fellow-helper to the truth.

Gaius is congratulated on *soul-health* as shown by his loyalty to truth and its representatives. Here again is a hint as to *service*. One may have a very quiet sphere—be no public speaker or prominent worker, but, by acting the host and the true giver, receive the prophet, help his work and share his reward. Matt. x. 41.

Diotrephes is held up as a warning, not for heresy, but for his ambition and selfishness. There are other ways of rending a church, beside doctrinal error. Demetrius is commended as a witness to the truth.

JUDE.

Key-word: KEPT. *Key-verse:* 21, 24.

THIS, the last of the Epistles, mainly addresses Hebrew converts, and hence assumes the familiarity of the reader with Old Testament history. It is *a warning against Apostasy. Faith* makes *faithful* saints, who, contending for the faith and persevering, are preserved by Grace and presented in Glory. The contrast is marked between those who *kept not* their first estate and *are kept* for judgment, and those who *keep themselves* and *are kept* from falling.

Apostasy is presented in representative examples: *Antinomians,* who turn gracious liberty into lascivious license; *unbelieving Israel* in the Exodus; *disobedient angels; lustful Sodomites; self-righteous Cain; greedy Balaam; presumptuous Korah;* and *blasphemous mockers.* All of us are either *reserved* for the Day of Condemnation, or *preserved* for the Day of Presentation.

If we *keep ourselves* in the Love of God, fighting for the faith, building up ourselves upon the faith, praying in the Holy Ghost and looking for the coming of the Lord, God will *keep us* (guard as with a garrison).

The author is Jude or Judas. Time 65-80 A.D.

DIVISIONS: I. 1, 2. Salutation.
II.: 3. The Exhortation.
III.: 4-16. Warning Examples.
IV.: 17-23. Secrets of Preservation.
V.: 24, 25. Grand Doxology.

REVELATION.

Key-word: REVELATION (ἀποκαλυψις). *Key verse:* I. 1.

Apocalypse is the opposite of *Mystery* (μυστηριον). The Books of Daniel and of John are closely linked, and from them with those of Isaiah, Ezekiel, and Zechariah, all Apocalyptic literature is constructed. Daniel cast light on the Former Days, between the Captivity and the Fall of Jerusalem; John, on the Last Days, from the Fall of the Holy City to the Second Coming of the Lord.

John probably wrote this book between Paul's death, 64 A.D. and his own, 98 A.D. Patmos, the scene of his exile, suggests much of the symbolism of the Apocalypse; on every side, the sea with the sound of many waters; the broad Grecian sky with its massive clouds and fearful storms; the mountain ranges of Asia Minor, encircling the seven churches, etc.

Apocalyptic prophecy is *essentially symbolic.*

Mysteries, having no analogy in earthly things or past events, demand *images* for their expression. But symbols are not themselves of necessity added mysteries, and in this case more than fifty of them are explained by their equivalents as found, not only in other Scriptures but in this book itself. Cf. xii. 9; xvi. 13, 14; xvii. 18, etc.

There appears here a *numerical system*. God is the God of order, number, proportion, in every province of creation, as seen in crystals, plants, and animal structure. And here numbers are used to express ideas. One is the number of Unity; two, of contrast or confirmation; three, of Trinity, and so of Godhead; four, of the world and creation; seven, which is the sum of three and four, the Union of Divine and human activity; twelve, the product of three and four, the human pervaded by the divine; and these numbers, *seven* and *twelve*, with *ten*, which is the sum of one, two, three, and four are numbers of completeness: while *five*, which is the half of ten, *six*, which stops short of seven, and *three and a half*, the half of seven, and a broken number, represent incompleteness, unrest, and disaster. It is a significant fact that 666, the number of perpetual unrest, is the number of the Beast; and 888, the number of eternal triumph, is the numerical equivalent of Jesus (Ἰησους).

There are *four systems* of *interpretation:* 1. The *Preterist*, which traces here Jewish history down to the Fall of Jerusalem and of Pagan Rome. 2. The *Presentist*, which finds here an outline of events during the whole period since the writing of the prophecy. 3. The *Futurist*, which refers it to events closely linked with the Second Coming of Christ. 4. The *Spiritual*, which regards the book as a Battle-scene where all the great leading forces of Evil are brought into line against Christ and His followers, for the last, great Conflict of the Ages. In this view the book is not so much a particular as a general prophecy, an outline which fits, more or less fully, various historic periods, and from which in every age the Church may learn what disguises the Devil assumes, against what foes within and without she needs to be on guard, and how sure is the Final Victory.

The *principal charm* of the Apocalypse is that it reveals *the End of all things*. On the one hand, *Evil* reaches its final and full development; all the forms of enmity toward God and godliness come to their awful ripeness in the Harlot, the False Prophet, the Beast, and the Dragon. But, on the other hand, the saints, under the lead of the "Seed of the Woman," achieve the victory, and all foes are put to rout forever. The Kingdom is established upon the ruins of all hostile powers and dominions, and the last Enemy, Death, is destroyed.

And so, *all things are made new.* Paradise Lost becomes Paradise Regained. Once more the Tree of Life is seen by the River of the Water of Life; once more the Tabernacle of God is with men; but the curse of sin that blasted the first Eden shall no more blight the second Eden. As we compare the opening of Genesis with the close of Revelation, we find that we have been following the perimeter of a Golden Ring,—the two extremities of human history meet; from the Creation and Eden with the Fall, we have at last come to the New Creation, and Paradise without a Fall. And so, as the Book of God closes, it fixes the last look of the reader upon the *Coming One* whose Personal Presence ($\pi\alpha\rho o \upsilon \sigma \iota \alpha$) is to be the signal for the Final Consummation of Victory and Blessedness!

"SURELY I COME QUICKLY!"

"AMEN!

"EVEN SO, COME, LORD JESUS!"

Druck:
Customized Business Services GmbH
im Auftrag der KNV-Gruppe
Ferdinand-Jühlke-Str. 7
99095 Erfurt